Dr. Stan Mars

Awake and Arise
The Dying of the American Church

A Call for Reformation to Revival

WESTBOW
P R E S S®
A DIVISION OF THOMAS NELSON
& ZONDERVAN

WestBow Press books may be ordered through booksellers or by contacting:

WestBow Press
A Division of Thomas Nelson & Zondervan
1663 Liberty Drive
Bloomington, IN 47403
www.westbowpress.com
1 (866) 928-1240

Unless otherwise noted, Scripture quotations taken
from the King James Version of the Bible.

Scripture quotations marked (NIV) are taken from the Holy Bible, New International Version®, NIV®. Copyright © 1973, 1978, 1984, 2011 by Biblica, Inc.™ Used by permission of Zondervan. All rights reserved worldwide. www. zondervan.com The "NIV" and "New International Version" are trademarks registered in the United States Patent and Trademark Office by Biblica, Inc.™

ISBN: 978-1-9736-7226-5 (sc)
ISBN: 978-1-9736-7227-2 (hc)
ISBN: 978-1-9736-7225-8 (e)

Library of Congress Control Number: 2019912283

Print information available on the last page.

WestBow Press rev. date: 09/05/2019

Contents

Acknowledgments

I want to give credit where credit is due for this work. First, I must thank God for all His inspiration and guidance in this project. I would never have even come up with the idea of this book or the contents without His blessings. I must have started about eight different books on the same subject, but they just weren't right, or the timing wasn't right. After much prayer and attempts, the information you will read in this book flowed out of me with very little effort on my part. All glory goes to God! I am blessed and I hope you will be blessed in the reading of this work.

Secondly, I am indebted forever to my wife, Vicki. She has stood by me from the early days of our sanctification and the beginning of this eight-year academic journey. I would have never completed this part of our journey without her love. She stood by me during the tough days of frustration and she was an inspiration to me during the good days of joy but always she stood with me and I will always be in her debt. I love you Vicki with all my heart.

I must thank Liberty University and all the men that guided me in my classes from my graduate classes to my doctorate degree. I want to thank the Falwell family for supporting Jerry Falwell Sr. to answer God's call on his life and allow God to build this incredible school to God's glory through him and his family. To the Falwell family, I want to share my deep love and appreciation, for following in their father's footsteps and have taken their rightful places in leadership to continue this vision! I, also, want to thank men like Dr. Rice, Dr. Dempsey, Dr. Hirschman, and Dr. McFarland. One man that I can't forget as he held such an amazing place in my heart is Dr. Charley Davidson. Charley has gone on to be with the Lord (may he rest in peace) but the impact he made on my life in such a short time, will forever have an imprint on my heart, and I will forever be indebted for his love and guidance. These men played a major part in my journey and without them I would have never accomplished this task. I am forever indebted!

Lastly, I want to thank all the men and women who, for whatever their reasons, rejected me, stood against me, and without cause hated me as they hated Jesus, as this caused me great pain but it drove me on to accomplish this work. You made it so clear the many reasons that the American Church was dying and in need of reformation and revival. You know who you are, and I thank you for rejecting me and the truth.

Introduction

Allow me to begin by saying that I love the church that is a church of God. God's House is a very special place for me and for me to experience God. However, allow me to tell you the truth, not all churches in America are a House of God. Many churches in America do not even allow Jesus Christ or the Holy Spirit inside the building. We know that schools, government offices, and legal facilities do not allow God in their buildings, well, many churches in America are the same. Let me be honest, you won't hear any leader of a church in America say that Jesus isn't invited, or the Holy Spirit doesn't lead their church. However, the proof is in the puddin' as we say in the south.

Allow me to explain the title of this book as it has great meaning and it comes from two places in the Bible. First, in the gospel of Mark, we find Jesus being requested to come to the home of one of the Jewish rulers of the synagogue who was named Jairus. Apparently, Jairus's daughter had become ill and was dying, so this Jewish leader who knew of Jesus, believed that Jesus could heal his daughter. At one point the servant of Jairus came and told him that it was too late, Jairus's daughter had died. Jesus continued and went to this man's house and they were all crying and making a lot of commotion in the house. In Mark 5:39, "and when He was come in, He saith unto them, why make ye this commotion, and weep? The damsel (child) is not dead, but sleepth." This is an amazing statement as everyone in the house knew she had died so to hear Jesus say this must have shocked them. The reality is that the people were right, and the child died but they didn't know what, or whom, had come into their home. Jesus knew she would be healed so he was speaking to them in the future tense. She was just sleeping to Jesus, but to man, she had died. This is very much like the Church of America. I believe that Jesus has spewed the church out, but there is hope that she can live again but only if she will change her path, confess, repent, and be forgiven. The last step is to become humbled and obedient to God to begin to do God's Church in God's Way! The Church of America is dying and may be dead, but to God, the Church of America is simply sleeping.

In Mark 5:41 - 42 we see that Jesus then goes to the child and says, "Talitha cumi; which is being interpreted, Damsel, (I say unto thee,) arise. And straightway the damsel arose and walked: for she was of the age of twelve years. And they were astonished with a great astonishment." Jesus brought her back to life and the people were shocked and amazed! This is what Jesus is saying to the Church of America. Church of America - Awake and Arise and live a life that is to bring glory to God and blessings to us. The Church of America must awaken to the truth that we are dying and when we accept this truth, we must be humbled and confess, repent, and be forgiven of our sins, and begin a life of obedience!

The second place in the Bible for the title comes from Ephesian 5:14, "Wherefore he saith, awake thou that sleepest, and arise from the dead, and Christ shall give thee light." This again is exactly what the Church of America must do; we must awaken to the truth of what we have done, and we must arise from the ashes and begin to serve an Almighty God in the way He requires of us. We must understand that modern day Christianity has little to do with the Bible and this is a truth we must turn from and turn to God for His mercy! If we ever want to be the light of Christ that is promised, we must allow God to change who we are.

Let me begin by saying, I learned a valuable lesson as I submitted my final paper (Thesis Project) to receive my Doctor of Ministry Degree. One of the men on the board that I defended my paper to made a wonderful and powerful statement as he said, "you say the American Church is dying, but my church isn't dying, we are loving others, making disciples, people are being saved and baptized all the time, so how is we are dying?" I didn't have an answer and he told me that I was speaking truth about most of the churches in America but not all the churches of America. What a powerful lesson I learned so I want you to know, and I say this in other places in this book, it is not ALL the Churches of America that I speak of, but most of them. So, as he was offended, and within his rights, as I didn't clearly state my position, I am clearly making this point now, when you read of the American Churches in this book, PLEASE, know I am speaking of most, or the majority, of churches. If your church is in obedience with the Word of God, then please read this book in hopes of helping other churches. However, if your church falls within the majority I speak of, don't look away or be offended but accept the truth and be moved by God to confess, repent, and move to obey Him. Enough said on that point.

Another saying we use in the south is that "you got too much cream in your puddin'" and that means that your story isn't making sense, or your story is very thin in truth. I was sitting in a court room in hopes of helping a person with my testimony when I heard the Judge say that in open court. I let out this loud laugh and then immediately felt bad as I looked around and everyone was looking at me. I had never heard that saying nor had I heard a saying of that nature made by an educated man. I knew I was now deep in the south! You will read many stories in this book about different elements of the American Church and I believe you will never say that my "puddin' has too much cream in it."

The last southern saying, I will introduce many of

you too that we use all the time is "I'm going to tell you how the cow eats the cabbage." This means that I'm going to tell you the truth, the whole truth, and nothing but the truth, whether you like it or not! Much of this book may offend and hurt many of you who have never given thought to the true condition of the church, and especially the church you attend. You will learn some staggering facts about the true condition of our churches, and I won't leave you wondering what to do or what needs to be done in my personal, and professional, opinion. I coached a lot of football teams in my lifetime and I had the honor of coaching at the high school, college, and the semi-professional levels. I would always tell the players right before a game – "tighten up those chin straps and get ready to hit and be hit today as this will be brutal." Allow me to borrow that line for this book. Please keep an open mind and heart as you read the truth and read this book cover to cover. It will be brutally honest, but it will also drive you to understand the truth, stand in the truth, and make the changes necessary to honor God but you will need to tighten up those chin straps!

The American Church is in deep trouble. The decline is staggering and has led us to understand that she isn't just in decline numerically, but she is gasping for her last breath. The main reason the church finds herself on her death bed is the sin of mankind. Man's sin has caused her to lose her way and why she was created by and for God. Have you ever heard the story that if you take a frog and place this frog into a boiling pot of water, the frog will immediately hop right out of the water due to the heat? However, if you take the same frog and place him in the lukewarm pot of water and then slowly increase the heat until it is boiling, the frog won't notice and will die a painful death. Is this what has happened to the American Church?

As you explore these truths with me on this journey, I again, want you to be prepared to learn some difficult truths. If you can accept these truths you will be able to make a stand for God to help bring the American Church to revival and good health if she will confess, repent, and begin the path of obedience to God. I'm afraid to say that if we do not act now, the church will die, and the wrath of God will replace her. I don't want my legacy to be a part of that scenario. Do you? Enjoy the journey and remember that if you are a child of God, there is hope! There is always hope in Jesus Christ. Our hope must always be in, and on, Jesus Christ as our Lord and Savior. We must be willing to bring glory to Him and this will bring blessings to us. He is our hope! May God Bless You and Your Family, the American Church, and the United States of America.

Chapter 1

The Journey for Truth Begins

"Therefore, if any man be in Christ, he is
a new creature: old things are passed away;
behold, all things are become new."
2 Corinthians 5:17

I grew up in a small southern town called West Memphis, Arkansas in the '60's. I know what you are thinking – man, this guy is old – and you would be right. However, being old isn't such a bad thing as I do have a lot of memories in the old memory bank. The problem is trying to withdraw from this bank at times is difficult. Don't let me kid you though, there are times I can't remember why I walked into a room. I think to myself, what did I come in here for? Then I think, why am I talking to myself? It can sometimes be like a dog chasing his tail. Well, as I speak with others my age and older, that is just a part of growing older. My father used to say before he passed that whoever called this part of life called the "golden age" was full of hooey. I still call this life a blessing from God as

I continue to learn and many times what I learn brings me a sadness. The fact that I am writing this book is a blessing, but it comes from a sadness that I had to learn. I have often struggled with God on why He chose me to write this book.

This book is written with great sadness concerning the truth about the Church of America. I wish it was different, but it is a book of truth. The truth that I had to learn, or should I say that I was given by God, is a truth that will bring great sadness to you if you receive it in the manner I am offering. However, if you struggle and fight the truth you may find that you will be in denial and anger at many points in your reading. I did not make this truth up, but this truth was given to me over time by God Himself. I had to see things that I had never seen before and experience things that I had to experience, so I could truly understand the impact of the truth. I want you to know that in my daily walk with God, I had to see things that broke my heart. I had to catch myself and ask, "God, is this really what you want me to see?" There were many times in my walk with God that I would scream out, "I have seen enough Lord, I know it is broken. I don't need to see anymore." It was that painful. I will say that I know God heard me every time, but God continued to show me so many different things, so I had the fullness of the big picture. I want to share the truth with you. Remember, I am just the simple messenger bringing a message to you that you probably will want to reject but I encourage you to keep your heart and mind open to this truth so you may be a part of the solution and not the problem.

As I said, I was a kid living in the south in the '60's. My life seemed simple, but I knew there were problems, but I wasn't old enough to understand. I remember attending church, but I remember we didn't go to church regularly. My family attended a Presbyterian church in West Memphis, Arkansas. Driving home from church my dad would offer the kids a dime for anyone who could remember what the sermon was on that day and I do remember receiving a dime occasionally. That was very exciting for me – a whole dime! I tell you this because I remember getting my dime for telling my dad that the message the preacher had given that day was on love. What my dad didn't know was that about everything that preacher spoke on the topic of love, I had never experienced in my family or my life.

I hate to tell you this, but if I don't, you won't get the whole picture and like my journey with God – you must get the whole picture. I was the product of a very violent and toxic home. I know what the meaning of domestic violence is and the power it has on a person's life. I am the youngest child in the family of four as I have two brothers and one half-sister. My mother and father had many problems that spilled over into all our lives that caused great pain to us all.

I have vivid memories of my father coming home drunk and my mother yelling, screaming, and then attacking him as he walked in the door. She would hit him and pull his hair and they would wrestle to the floor as I stood there screaming for them to stop fighting. Tears that I never thought would stop. In one fight, my father had my mother's arm twisted behind her back and he ultimately broke her thumb. That was bad, but the next day I remember my mother teaching me to lie for the first time in my life. She taught me to tell anyone that asked that she fell off a stool in the kitchen and to lie and not tell anyone about my mother and father fighting. I didn't understand anything, but I did know I was being taught to lie. I didn't know at the time – my own mother was teaching me to sin.

My mother and father fought in this manner each week, so I grew accustomed to this event. I hated it every time, but I knew it would continue to happen. The only difference was the severity of each fight. Most I only heard from my bed and that was terrifying. I would hear the yelling, cussing, and screaming and it sounded like they were killing each other. As a young boy, that was very traumatic. I also had the privilege to see many of their displays of hatred toward each other and that too had a heavy impact on my life. I remember one time the fighting was so bad that my sister huddled us boys into our bedroom and we hid under a desk together. I never forgot the feeling of her trying to protect us from the pain we all suffered.

I will spare you more memories of my youth, but it is just

safe to say that many of them are not pleasant. To say my mother suffered from anger issues is an understatement. Her explosive anger wasn't confined and limited to just my father. I also witnessed her horrific displays of anger as she would explode on others. She also suffered from anger issues, severe depression, and struggled with a form of mental illness. In her defense, she lost her mother and father at the young age of four and six respectfully and was raised by her family members. She was passed around the family like a hot potato, living with different people for short periods of time and her past caused her great pain in her life. This never gave her license to be abusive, but it does give insight into how hurt people can hurt people.

Now you have a glimpse into my life as a young person growing up in the south. The '60's was a violent time for our country also. As I stated previously, I lived in West Memphis, Arkansas just across the bridge from Memphis, Tennessee and I was bussed to a school in Marion, Arkansas, about five miles from West Memphis. Marion was a very small town and though it felt like a lot of kids went to Marion school, I bet we didn't have 100 kids or so at that time. The entire school consisted of all kids from each grade 1 – 12 in the same building. At one point, I remember that they built a new elementary school and we were separated from the older kids until I believe we reached the seventh grade. The "big" school in my eyes was the high school that housed the kids from the

7 – 12 grades. That was a scary place as I had heard that they would de-pants the young kids and run the pants up the flag pole. I remember that I would always be on the look out for any older kids as I was terrified that my pants would go up the pole! Awww, the school memories of a kid!

I remember my first worldly memory and that was when President Kennedy was shot and killed. I was sitting in class in the elementary school and a lady opened the door to our classroom. She had tears running down her cheeks and she stepped into the classroom and said that we were being dismissed from school, so we were to get our things together to get on the bus. She followed that with the stunning news of the shooting of the President of the United States. I remember I was very sad, but I really didn't know why I was sad. I mean, I didn't know this guy, but it seemed like a very sad time. However, I do remember they closed the school for a few days, and we stayed home. I was glued to our black and white television set for hours watching the funeral and all the stories. That brought the sadness home to my heart in a big way.

Another powerful time in my young life was, I remember as I was sitting in the Marion gym watching a play, the gym lights suddenly came up in the middle of the play and an announcement that Martin Luther King, Jr. had just been shot and killed. I remember this time to be in the evening for some reason. I know he was shot in the middle of the day and maybe it took time for the riots to spill over toward the West Memphis/Marion area. Anyway, they stopped the play and sent us home from the school as they said that they were beginning to riot in Memphis, Tennessee. I remember thinking that I don't know this guy, but it seemed sad that a guy was killed. I had no knowledge of Martin Luther King, Jr. at all. I didn't know anything about his struggles and fight for equality and the Civil Rights Movement. I was just too young. The impact on my heart was the same however, I was sad this guy was shot and killed.

I do remember watching the television and they broke into programming to tell us that the Arkansas National Guard was at the bridge defending Arkansas from the riots in Memphis. I remember that a large group of black men were attempting to cross the bridge into Arkansas and the National Guard sent shots across the bridge and said they wouldn't allow them to cross into Arkansas. The ringing of a bullet off the metal bridge is a vivid memory but I can't be sure how accurate that memory is in my mind. I do remember being so proud of the National Guard though. They defended me and I always wondered if I was so moved by their action because of my home life. Domestic violence will always leave a child very insecure and unsafe. The actions of the Arkansas National Guard defending me made me feel safe. That is so strange isn't it?

I hope you now understand why I didn't understand the message of love preached by a man in church. He spoke of this love that I had never experienced. It sounded good but I remember I could never relate to the truth he spoke. I had never felt this love, nor had I experienced the feeling of love from another except maybe that night I was huddled with my sister under a desk. Was that love or just connected to another person in fear – I will never know – but I did get that dime!

It seemed at the time all my friends went to a church. We had a large group of friends that would mostly hang out and play sports. I remember one of my best friends was Dr. Jack (Buddy) Greenoe and he was very athletic and just a cool guy. He attended Calvary Baptist Church and he was a catcher on their baseball team. I too was a catcher on a Boys Club team and I always asked my mom if I could go to Buddy's church and join their baseball team but for some reason I wasn't allowed. I had always noticed as I hung out at Buddy's house that it was so peaceful. He had an older sister, Carolyn, and she was sweet but never had time for us boys. She was in high school, so it wasn't strange she didn't want to hang out with us. However, I always noticed how she was sweet and loving toward Buddy. Buddy's mom and dad were very nice people. His dad worked a lot, so I never got to know him very well, but I did love his mom. As a matter of fact, I had the honor to reunite with her in her last days/years on earth before she passed from this life. I learned she was in the hospital not far from our home and my wife and I drove down to visit her. She didn't know me at first as it had only been about forty years since I had seen her but as soon as I told her my name, her eyes lit up and a big smile crossed her face and she threw open her arms and hugged me. It was a special time. I digress.

We lived in West Memphis for about six or seven years of my young life and it was when I was thirteen that we moved. My father was a crop-dusting pilot who had owned his own flying service. I remember he had this big plane that had two wings. One wing was on top of the other wing and it was painted in a bright yellow. I didn't get to go out to his work or to see the plane much, maybe a few times, but I loved going out there. A sad thought as I write this book is that I don't ever remember that he took me for a plane ride. For what ever reason, I was always proud of my father and his work. However, one day I came home from school and my mom said we were moving to Detroit, Michigan! My dad had taken a job as a Lear Jet pilot for some company. I remember always wondering how someone moves from this bi-winged old plane to these fancy jets, but my dad did, and he was good at it. He ultimately owned his own Lear Jet business. He was never home which was fine by me, but I remember that I had no idea where this Detroit was, but it didn't sound like I was going to like it. I was right!

So I don't bore you to death, I will give you the highlights of my teenage years. Once we moved to Detroit, the physical fighting between my mother and father seemed do die out. My father was never home until real late at night and he left real early in the morning. As

I remember back, I don't believe my father and I ever had a conversation until I was about thirty years old. He was a very cold and distant man until he retired and as he got older, he began to soften in his old age.

I became a very angry young man. We moved many times over my remaining school years. I believe I attended five different schools in five years' time. For a young person who had not been offered any security and safety in his life, and then to continue to uproot him from the few stable things in his life, will cause a child to grow up very angry. I lived for many years simply angry at the world. I could never put my finger on the reasons why I was so angry as I didn't have the ability to understand, but I lived out my anger.

First, I was a very talented athlete in several sports. I found that through sports I would have the ability to make friends in all the schools I had to attend. People seemed to be drawn to me and being a good athlete helped me in many ways to cope with the great pain I was living through. As a kid in Arkansas, I was a state track champion and I was drawn to the sport of football though I wasn't as big as a minute. Once we moved to the Detroit, Michigan area, I continued my desire to play sports. I also found it helped with increasing the pool of girls that I could date! That was such a great plus in my life. As a freshman in school, I was the record holder and undefeated champion in the 60 and the 100-yard dash. As a Sophomore in high school I ran on and won the state championship for the 440-relay team as well as finished fifth in the state for the 100-yard dash. That was pretty good for a kid from Arkansas living in Michigan! The problem was that I suffered the first defeat of my life in the 100-yard dash in that state meet. I lost to an incredible athlete who at the time was a senior in school. His name was Marshall Dill! I was in the lane next to him and he was a grown man! He was a black man with a full beard, and I thought he had to be seven feet tall! He scared me to death, and I was so humbled to be in a race against his talent! He smoked me!

The real problem wasn't that I lost the race. Though I had lived many years undefeated, it was hard to accept. The real problem was one no one would have been able to see. Though my father and I never had a conversation and he wasn't a part of my life, I still would seek his approval. He never liked sports and never cared if I played sports. He always thought of me playing sports as childish and a waste of time. That always hurt me. What he said to me the day of this state event crushed me. As he was leaving for work, he leaned into the kitchen where I was sitting eating a bowl of Cheerios, and said, "don't you have a track meet today?" Shocked he would even ask me a question and hoping he would want to come to one of my races, I uttered, "yes sir." He said, "well, don't get beat by one of those black guys!" He left the house after that statement. Needless to tell you this, but it took about twenty years for me to understand my pain.

I did lose to a great athlete who happened to be a black man. However, in my head, I always remembered his words, and I did lose. I never ran track again! I did continue to play two years of high school football but that was only as an expression of anger. I had the honor to play for a young high school coach at the time and he went on in his career to become a great college coach. His name is Lloyd Carr and he became the University of Michigan head coach. Coach Carr and I butted heads all the time in my high school career. One time he was yelling at me so bad that I took off my helmet and threw it at him and hit him right in the chest. I felt horrible but I couldn't fight my pride. Amazingly, Coach Carr didn't discipline me and nothing was ever said about that event. He will never know how much I needed him in my life.

I began to smoke and drink at a young age. I remember standing on a street corner with a friend who was smoking a cigarette and he offered a smoke. I accepted and I ended up smoking for thirty years. I would go to a friend's home after school and many people would come over to her house and we would drink every night. I stole a car from their house one day and drove to Canada and bought two cases of beer and came home and dropped the car off at their house. I never knew if anyone knew I stole their car. It was a 1964 Ford Mustang, 3 speed shifts on the floor which meant I had to push in the clutch and shift gears to drive it. I had never driven a stick shift and I didn't even have a driver's license, but I just wanted to go to Canada and buy beer. I had no job, so I don't even remember how I got money to buy beer – guessing I stole that too. I didn't know it then, but I was an alcoholic in high school. I was in great pain and no one would help me. I was an angry young man.

I was about to graduate from high school and my mother informed me that I would have to have a full-time job, or I would not be allowed to live in her house. That was a nice way of saying that she threw me out of the house. I applied to all the factories in Detroit in hopes of finding a job, but I was only seventeen and didn't realize that no one would hire me until I reached the age of eighteen. I couldn't find a full-time job and she was going to throw me out of the house, so I joined the U.S. Army! I had never felt safe or secure in my life and now I was leaving and joining the Army. This couldn't be good! It was a blessing on one hand and a curse on the other. I was very intelligent, so I was awarded a great job in the Army as a Congressional Investigator at Fort Hood, Texas. I got married to my high school sweetheart and life was good. However, it turned bad quickly. She got pregnant and lost our child. That caused us great pain. Then I received orders to go to Germany. We packed up and she went home to live with her parents, and I went to Germany. In Germany, I smoked a lot of dope and was introduced to hard drugs. Ultimately, I became a heroin addict as well as an alcoholic. I came home to America a drug addict and a drunk. This was during the Vietnam War, so I guess I just fit the stereotype for the time.

I immediately got a divorce and even before my divorce was final, I got engaged! I was so out of control looking back it scares me. I got remarried quickly and we had three children, but marriage ended in divorce also. She never knew I was addicted to drugs or alcohol. It took me until I was sixty years old to admit I was an addict and an alcoholic, so I wasn't surprised she never had a clue. That divorce caused me great pain and still I never associated that pain with my anger. At this time in my life, I was thirty-five years old and needed help. This is how I finally met this person called Jesus Christ.

I finally hit my bottom in life and cried out to this God of Love that I didn't know. I had enough information about Him that told me He would save me from drowning in this life, so I called out to Him. To my amazement, He was there and answered my cries! I felt His presence and I knew that I needed to confess I was a sinner and repent of those sins to be forgiven. I confessed, repented, and He was faithful to forgive me. *I WAS SAVED*!

This is where this journey gets interesting. A few nights after I was saved, I went to bed and I wish I could tell you I was in deep prayer or in a deep Bible study, but it was just another night and I went to bed. I had just shut off my bedroom light and climbed into bed. Then I noticed how bright the red numbers were that illuminated the time from my alarm clock were in the room. That was the only light in the room. I closed my eyes and began to drift off to sleep. This is where it got weird. As I was laying there drifting off to sleep, I feel this power enter my room. It felt like a tornado type power. This power felt like it had a high powerful wind that was circling the room like a tornado. Where were flashes of light like small but powerful lightening strikes. It was like a powerful storm was in my bedroom. Now I challenge you to get your head around that if you were in my bed? I was surprised and shocked as well as scared to death. I kept looking at the walls where I could see the silhouettes of the pictures were hanging expecting them to be flying off the walls – but they remained completely still. Was this a dream? Was this a nightmare? What was happening to me?

Though it seemed like hours, it was only but a few moments, and it happened. There standing at the foot of my bed was a man. In a flash, the room was lit up in a warm glowing light and He was standing there. He wasn't doing anything or saying anything. He just stood there. Another amazing element of this meeting was that I couldn't look at His face. I saw His build and His hair, but not His face. I, to this day, don't know if I didn't have the power to look at His face or in humbleness, I knew I didn't deserve to look at His face, but either way, I didn't look at His face.

I do remember that I began to slide off my bed and kneel by the bed with my head buried in the mattress. After a few moments, I felt that wasn't appropriate and I moved to a prostrate position on the floor of my bedroom with my face buried in the carpet on the floor. I use the word prostrate as it truly defines how I felt at that moment. The word prostrate means to lie face down in humbleness and acknowledgment of our total unworthiness. I remember that I couldn't bury my face deep enough into that carpet. I did sneak a glance upward and Jesus was just standing there in His warmth and love. Another peek and it was completely dark. Jesus left quietly and silently.

I remember looking up slowly and wondering what had just happened in my life. Could that have really happened? Then in a moment I was brought back to my reality of being in my dark bedroom laying on the floor. I will never forget what happened at that moment. I jumped up and went to my walk-in closet and grabbed my 9-iron out of my golf bag. I quickly headed to the door and slowly opened it to only reveal a dark hallway that led to my living room. I was calling out asking "Who is here?" Totally naked and armed with a 9-iron, I crept through the apartment looking for an intruder and flipping on lights as I went. All the doors and windows were closed and locked. There was nothing out of place.

Then it hit me – what an idiot I was! Standing naked in my apartment with a 9-iron thinking someone broke in only to find nothing. I have never felt more like a human being than at that moment. The need to understand what just happened to me was a powerful force and I just couldn't wrap my head around meeting Jesus Christ!

There is a funny story in this story, and I will share it with you. A few days had past and I called and shared this story with my best friend Dave, and he was blown away but then he said something very funny. He said, "why did you grab your 9-iron, you know you can't hit anything with that club!" I will never forget how we laughed. Then we got back to the experience and it was a powerful moment for us both.

I wish I could tell you that was the end of the story, but I went back to bed and fell asleep and got up and went to work the next day. I felt awkward like a had a great secret, but everyone knew. The truth was that no one had a clue except one person. At the time, I was the director of admissions for a private college and every day I would stand outside of my office and greet the students going to class to encourage them and simply welcome them to school for the day. On this day, I was so off balance, I decided to just slip in my office earlier than usual and close my office door so no one would bother me. I just didn't know what to say had happened to me.

I thought every student had gone past my office to class and I began to feel better and breath a sigh of relief when suddenly, a person, who didn't knock on my office door, just opened my door and stuck their head in the door. It was a very close student/friend named Tammy. She looked at me and instantly pushed the door open and stepped inside with a look of horror on her face. I remember I looked intently at her and, in an almost shout, said, "get in here and shut the door." She did close the door and looked at me and I was terrified by her look. She had lost all the color in her face and she said, "you have been in the presence of Jesus, haven't you?" I will never forget that I looked at her and said, "how do you know this?"

She smiled at me and said, "relax you are alright, but I have to tell you I see this light blue aura around you, and it is making your hair look white." She told me that it was the most beautiful light blue color she has ever seen, and it was so soothing to her. I was almost frantic as I asked her about my white hair as I said, "you don't mean I look like Moses coming off the mountain, do you?" She laughed out loud and said no, it isn't white it just looks kind of white next to the blue aura.

Many people that day didn't say they saw the blue aura, but they did say, "what is different about you today?" Only a few could see the aura around me but only Tammy knew what that aura represented and knew what had happened. To this day, I miss talking to Tammy as our paths separated and I lost touch with her. She had a wonderful connection to Jesus Christ and will always be considered a blessing and a friend in my life.

This was my beginnings as a human being and my new beginnings as a child of God. I was so excited to begin my journey with God and immediately after I was reborn and my soul safely restored into the image of God, I began my journey to become a disciple. The first thing

I did was receive my baptism and then began reading the Bible. I will never forget that once I picked up the Bible and began reading in Genesis, I was hooked and over the next six months I read and studied His Word in a manner like a starving child and I just couldn't get enough of His Word.

I spoke with my father who by this time had become a professing believer in Jesus Christ and he offered to me an opportunity to begin a Bible course from Liberty University called the Wilmington Bible Institute. I received this course and in less than six months I had completed the course and received straight A's. I had never been very good in my academic pursuit but in this program, with the power of the Holy Spirit, I couldn't be stopped. I ate it up!

Now the real test of my life began. I was to begin to seek becoming a church goer. What was the right church? What was the right denomination? How does one begin to search out the right church? I had so many questions and so many people offered their opinions. In the end, I trusted God for His guidance and the search began.

The problem was that in every church I was to attend, there were glaring problems. I knew I was a protestant person. Was I a Baptist? Was I a Presbyterian? Was I a Methodist? The list grew long, and my research of each denomination was extensive. I attended many churches, but I could never find one that was the right fit for me personally. I didn't know it then, but the problem didn't lie with me but in the church itself. However, since I didn't have the truth about the church, I felt so guilty as there were many times, I just grew tired and would stop going to church for a season. I would feel bad and then catch my breath and begin my quest again – to no avail. I can't tell you how many times I felt like it had to be me and that made me feel horrible.

This quest would continue over a twenty-year span. I would join a church and stay a year or so and become so bored and unchallenged and then I would leave in search of another church. I must tell you that I knew I wasn't looking for the perfect church as I knew when I walked into that church it would become imperfect. I wasn't a church hopper just hopping from one church to another out of disliking one thing or another.

I will tell you that even when I became a pastor at my first church, I became so unhappy. I had been the pastor of this church for over three years. I was driving home after a service and I looked at my wife and said, "If this is all there is as a pastor, I need to find another career." I couldn't believe I was saying that, but my spirit was never at rest. God continued to speak to my spirit and force me out of my comfort zone and make me question what I was doing.

That is when I began another academic search and again returned to Liberty University. In a few short years, I had received my Master of Theological Studies Degree, a Master of Divinity Degree, and amazingly, my Doctor of Ministry Degree. In this pursuit laid the answers I had been seeking for so many years! I want to share them with you, and I hope you will be able to accept the truth and that this truth will move you to stand up and become a part of the solution.

I also hope you have a better understanding of the person I was, the person I became, and know that I am a broken and flawed human being like many of my readers. My soul has been restored to the image of God and I am growing daily into the likeness of Jesus Christ and this is to His glory and my blessings. I am just less broken and less flawed as I was when I was in the world separated from the person of Jesus Christ. As you read this book, I will continue to share many different experiences I have had with God. I felt that this was the best way to begin our journey to understand what I have learned in relation to God, His church, and His people, and myself. I truly hope this book will be a blessing for you and your family. Now, onward into the truth!

Chapter 2

"The Dying of the American Church"

"For the wages of sin is death;"
Romans 6: 23

Let me be honest with you as we begin this journey – the American Church is in a death spiral! Most churches in America are just going through the motions and the leadership continues to turn away from the truth. We have known for many years that most of the American Churches have been in a very steep and dangerous decline and now most are in a death spiral. Let me also point out the word "MOST." Most American Churches are not only in decline but are dying the slow death. If your church isn't included in this majority, please open your heart to the truth and be moved to help other churches that are dying and help them find reformation and revival. Allow me to state that I love the God's church of America but, like God, I have had great despair on how we *DO CHURCH*. Please don't label me as anti-church but understand that, like Martin Luther who felt compelled to stand against the Catholic Church and fought for reformation, I must stand against most of the American Churches and fight for *TRUE REFORMATION AND REVIVAL*. Let us examine the facts on why I would make a statement that most churches are dying as we speak.

The American Church is in crisis, and is slowly dying, as church growth has plateaued or declined. Daniel Sanchez states, "Approximately 80% of all churches in North America have reached a plateau or are declining."[1] There are hundreds of thousands of churches in the United States of America that are in crisis. According to Scott Thumma and Dave Travis, "in 2007 there were 335,000 churches in America."[2] In the United States of America, of the 335,000 churches, 80% of those churches are either in plateau or decline, which would bring a mathematical calculation of 268,000 churches in America would be either flat lined or declining. This is a staggeringly high number of churches in crisis. One major reason for the decline of church growth is found in lack of conversion of the lost to Jesus Christ. George Barna says, "The evangelical church in America is losing the battle to effectively bring Jesus Christ into the lives of the unsaved population....Since 1980, there has been no growth in the proportion of the adult population that

---

[1] Daniel R. Sanchez, *Church Planting Movements in North America* (Fort Worth, TX: Church Starting Network, 2007), 18.

[2] Scott Thumma and Dave Travis, *Beyond Megachurch Myths: What We Can Learn from America's Largest Churches* (San Francisco, CA: Jossey-Bass Publishers, 2007), 1.

can be classified as "born again" Christian."[3] Hundreds of thousands of churches in America are in crisis due to their lack of conversion growth. Thom Rainer says, "So the church began its death march. Family by family the church declined. Of course, the membership of the church grew older. Those who once lived in the community represented the oldest of the members, and no younger families replace them."[4] Church decline leads to the ultimate death march for the church. George Barna says, "The actively churched are those who attend church regularly, usually once a month or more often. Based on our 2014 tracking data, this group represents 49 percent of the adult population."[5] This leaves fifty-one percent of American adults do not attend church even once a month. Thom and Joani Schultz state, "There's no easy way to say this, but it needs to be said: The American Church is Broken."[6] A staggering statistic is offered by Steven Hewitt as he states, "From 1990 to 2000, the combined membership of all Protestant denominations in the U.S. declined by almost 5 million members (9.5 percent) while

---

[3] George Barna, *Marketing the Church: What They Never Taught You About Church Growth* (Colorado Springs, CO: NavPress, 1991), 21.

[4] Thom Rainer, *Autopsy of a Deceased Church: 12 Ways to Keep yours Alive* (Nashville, TN: B&H Publishing Group, 2014), 26.

[5] George Barna and David Kinnaman, Editors, *Churchless: Understanding Today's Unchurched and How to Connect with Them.* (Carol Stream, IL: Tyndale House Publishers, Inc. 2014), 7.

[6] Thom Schultz and Joani Schultz, *Why Nobody Wants to Go to Church Anymore: And How 4 Acts of Love Will Make your Church Irresistible* (Loveland, CO: Group. 2013), 5.

the U.S. population increased by 24 million (11 percent)."[7] Even though the population increased substantially over this time frame, millions left the church. In relation to people leaving the church, many churches are closing their doors each year. According to Thumma, "Every year more than 4,000 of them close their doors forever… and four out of five Americans say they're sure God exists and identify themselves with a faith group. But less than half of them even attend church."[8] According to T. Clegg and T. Bird, they state that fewer churches per 10,000 exist today than existed in 1920."[9] Obviously, the above information is a problem for the church of America and it leads to the revelation of another issue that is` problematic for the church.

The Problem is Simple: SIN

Most churches in America are not in the process of making disciples. I must tell you that in conducting my research for my Thesis Project in ministry (or you would probably better know this work as a Dissertation which is in the Ph.D. program) I spoke to many pastors and leaders concerning this very issue. I must tell you that I was shocked at their responses.

---

[7] Steven Hewitt. "Why the church is dying in America." *Christian Computing Magazine. July, 2012. 4.*

[8] Scott Thumma, "A health Checkup of U.S. Churches" by Hartford Institute for Religion Research, (presentation, Future of the Church Summit from Group Publishing, Loveland, CO, October 22, 2012). 4.

[9] T. Clegg and T. Bird, *Lost in America* (Loveland, CO: Group Publishing, 2001), 30.

I began by offering an area we could both agree so their defenses didn't go up and stop further discussion. I began with Matthew 28: 19-20 which Jesus states, "Therefore go, and make disciples of all nations, baptizing them in the name of the Father and of the Son and of the Holy Spirit, and teaching them to obey everything I have commanded you. And surely, I am with you always, to the very end of the age" (NIV). Every leader/pastor agreed that we have been commanded by Jesus to "Go and make disciples." Though we had to work to get an agreement on the understanding of the word disciples, ultimately, we did agree.

I then would ask them if their church, under their leadership, was making disciples. A few of them said yes but once I pointed out to them that preaching and Sunday School was two of the lowest forms of discipleship, they agreed that they, nor their church, was in the active pursuit of making disciples. Once we had that established, I guided them to this question – "If you are not obeying Jesus Christ in this commandment, are you not in sin?" After further discussion, to a man, the answer was that they were in sin for failing to obey the commandment.

A few of them had to be offered a scenario that would fit the moment as they struggled to acknowledge the truth about being in sin. I slowly said that if a man who was a member of their church came to him and confessed, he was having an affair on his wife and was hoping you could help him, what would they say to him? To a man, they all agreed that they would help him understand he is living in sin and needed to confess, repent, and seek forgiveness. I followed that with the fact they admitted to me they were in sin for not making disciples and – WATCH THIS – to a man, they all said they were not interested in confessing, repenting, or seeking forgiveness for their sinful actions. THESE WERE PASTORS FROM THE LOCAL CHURCHES IN OUR AREA!!!! BOOM!

According to George Barna, "My study of discipleship in America has been eye-opening. Almost every church in our country has some type of discipleship program or set of activities, but stunningly few churches have a church of disciples."[10] As stated above, the main reason leading to the failure of the making of disciples can be found in disobedience to follow the commandments of God and this is sin. I also like how the King James Version states this scripture as Jesus, in the Great Commission, commands His disciples to "Go ye therefore, and teach all nations, baptizing them in the name of the Father, and of the Son, and of the Holy Ghost: Teaching them to observe all things whatsoever I have commanded you: and, lo, I am with you always, even unto the end of the world. Amen."[11]

---

[10] George Barna, *Growing True Disciples: New Strategies for Producing Genuine Followers of Christ.* (Colorado Springs, CO: WaterBrook Press, 2001), 20.
[11] Matthew 28:19–20.

Sin # 1: The Sin of Not Making Disciples

I wanted to break down for you what I see as a multiple layer of sins in the American Church. The first sin that has caused the death spiral of the church is in rejecting the words of Jesus Christ. We have chosen a path of disobedience to Christ instead of being humbled and obeying Him in our service.

I also want to share with you what I believe is an important point on this issue. In the church leadership we do not have, nor do we accept, a complete understanding of the meaning of the word "disciple." When we struggle over the terminology of a word, it causes division and a lack of understanding. The church had, and has, a responsibility to come together as a body of Christ and set forth the same terminology so the teaching of this subject can be accepted by all. However, in lieu of that ever happening, allow an old man to offer his best definition, which is borrowed from two very intelligent men of God, of the word "disciple." This is the best definition of the word "disciple" that I have ever come across and I will share it with you.

> **"A disciple is a person who has trusted Christ for salvation and has *surrendered* completely to Him. He or she is committed to practicing the spiritual disciplines in**

community and developing to their full potential for Christ and His mission."[12]

If you can accept this definition of "disciple" then it will be a little easier to follow the logic of this book. Christ commanded us to make disciples and now we can understand the difference between a disciple of Jesus and a follower of Jesus. Both must be followers of Jesus, but the disciple is one who is "surrendered" to Christ and will accept not only all His teachings but the full leadership of God the Holy Spirit. To make this point, we look to the Word and we find, "From this time many of his disciples turned back and no longer followed him." [13] The words disciple and follower are used interchangeably in the New Testament so we see that these who turned away were truly just simply followers of Jesus and once they heard a teaching that they could not understand or accept, they rejected Jesus and turned away from Him. The American Church has become that same group as those seen in the previous scripture as they have rejected the teachings of Jesus Christ to go and make disciples of Jesus Christ.

Jesus commands His church to first go into the world and share the gospel and baptize the new believers, which is the process of evangelizing. Next, Jesus commands His church to teach others and help them grow into the

---

[12] Dave Earley & Rod Dempsey, *Disciple Making Is…: How to Live the Great Commission with Passion and Confidence.* (Nashville, TN: B&H Publishing Group, 2013). 28.
[13] John 6: 66 (NIV)

likeness of Christ, which is the process of discipleship. A person cannot become a disciple until they have been reborn by the blood of Jesus Christ and by the grace of God. A person cannot grow into the likeness of Jesus Christ until he/she has had the image of God restored on their soul.

However, Rainer says, "The deceased church, somewhere in its history, forgot to act upon the Great Commission. So, they stopped going. And making disciples. And baptizing them. And teaching them."[14] Failure to follow the commandment of Jesus Christ in reaching others is sin. According to Walter Elwell, "In the biblical perspective, sin is not only an act of wrong doing but a state of alienation from God."[15] Being separated and alienated from God due to sin causes man to lose his focus on his responsibility to God. Thom Rainer makes this clear as he says, "One of the main reasons many Christians do not share their faith is simply explained by the word disobedience. Spiritual lethargy takes place when we fail to obey him. The problem for many Christians is that they are not growing spiritually, and lack of spiritual growth inevitably leads to a diminished desire to share Christ with others."[16] David Platt understands the need for obedience as he states, "First, from the outset you

---

[14] Rainer, *Autopsy of a Deceased Church*, 41.

[15] Walter A. Elwell, ed. *Evangelical Dictionary of Theology.* 2nd ed. (Grand Rapids, MI: Baker Academic, 2001), 1103.

[16] Thom S. Rainer, *the unchurched next door: Understanding Faith Stages as Keys to Sharing Your Faith* (Grand Rapids, MI: Zondervan, 2003), 217.

need to commit to believe whatever Jesus says…then second you need to commit to obey what you have heard. The gospel does not prompt you to mere reflection; the gospel requires a response…'What Shall I Do?"[17] The result of sin is that others are not being converted to Jesus Christ and as Jim Putman says, "Our churches make few converts."[18] According to Jon Tyson, "For a nation that has always prided itself on spiritual foundations, it becomes profoundly unsettling when nearly two-thirds of eighteen to twenty-nine year old's with a Christian upbringing walk out of the church - perhaps never to return…59% of Millennials who grew up in the church have dropped out at some point."[19] This is a huge number that gives credible evidence that many of the youth of this generation did not receive conversion to Jesus Christ as they have dropped out and ceased attending church. Tyson also states that 70% of GenX and Millennials combined say they find God elsewhere other than church.[20] Also, an interesting point of view of an atheist is offered by Larry Taunton as he states, "Christianity is something that if you really believed it, it would change your life and you would want to change the lives of others. I haven't seen too much of

---

[17] David Platt, *Radical: Taking Your Faith Back from the American Dream.* (Colorado Springs, CO: Multnomah, 2010), 20-21.

[18] Jim Putman, *Real-life discipleship: building churches that make disciples* (Colorado Springs, CO: NavPress, 2010), 10.

[19] Jon Tyson, *Sacred Roots: Why the Church Still Matters* (Grand Rapids, MI: Zondervan. 2013), 31.

[20] Tyson, *Sacred Roots,* 73.

that."[21] Thus, it seems clear that the conversion growth rate in the church of America is virtually flat-lined.

How many churches have you attended or even the home church you attend presently, have you seen a person accepting Jesus Christ as their Lord and Savior lately? If you attend a church that offers an altar call at the end of the sermon, how lonely is that preacher who stands there knowing no one is leaving their seat to come forth to profess Jesus as their Lord. As a minister who offers altar calls, I can tell you this, that time for me was one of the most lonely and unfulfilling times for me as a preacher. Let me ask you this question – How many people have come to your church, not from a transfer in from another church, but from becoming reborn in Christ Jesus and walked the aisle to profess this new life in your church? One a week? One a month? One a year? God says in the Bible, "The Lord is not slack concerning his promise, as some men count slackness; but is longsuffering to us-ward, not willing that any should perish, but that all should come to repentance." [22] God doesn't want any soul to not return to Him in heaven but knows man will reject Him.

However, many souls today are on the path to hell because the American Church will not obey Jesus Christ and share the love of Christ with others so they can be

---

[21] Larry Alex Taunton, "Listening to young Atheists: Lessons for a Stronger Christianity," *The Atlantic,* June 6, 2013, http://www.theatlantic.com/national/archive/2013/06/listening-to-young-atheists-lessons-for-a-stronger-christianity/276584/.

[22] 2 Peter 3: 9

connected to the Father through Christ Jesus. The blood of hundreds of thousands, maybe millions, of men and women are on the hands of the leaders of the American Church! If you are a leader/pastor of an American Church who is not making disciples, will you RIGHT NOW, stop your reading, and kneel before God and confess you are a sinner in need of the loving forgiveness of Jesus Christ for your sins in disobedience – repent by turning away from your sins and to God and be forgiven. In the Bible it states clearly, "If we confess our sins, He is faithful and just to forgive us our sins, and to cleanse us from all unrighteousness."[23]

May I also say that if you are simply a lay person in leadership, or for that matter, a person who attends or is a member of a local New Testament Church, this also applies to you. You also have a responsibility to go forth and make disciples and not sit and wait for your pastor to stop sinning. Let this truth embrace your heart and move you to stand up for Christ and become the solution to the problem.

Sin # 2: The Sin of Not Loving Others

If the church is in sin of disobedience and not in the process of making disciples, we may come to understand that this is even deeper. If we don't care about following the commandments of God, it could be stated that this

---

[23] 1 John 1: 9

reflects on our relationship to God. My question is this, do we truly love God? I will illuminate only two very important statements of God on this issue. First, we find that God tells Israel "Hear, O Israel: the LORD our God, the LORD is one. Love the LORD your God with all your heart and with all your soul and with all your strength."[24] When one boils down the entire Bible into one word, they would find that word is LOVE. We should be moved to love God and be in a relationship with Him. If we are to be in a healthy, loving and intimate relationship with God, we are to keep His commandments. Jesus says "IF ye love me, keep my commandments."[25] Clearly, we are not keeping His commandments as the church is in direct disobedience to God. Also, as I referenced the facts stated by Barna earlier, could this be why people are not truly being reborn as they are not accepting the lordship of Jesus Christ as a part of the plan of salvation. If the church rejects the lordship of Jesus, by their actions of disobedience, then the congregation may be missing this fact also. Let me state that the lordship of Jesus means He has earned the right to be your Master, Owner, and Ruler. We are to be in obedience to the Lord Jesus but if we remove this from the equation, as the church has apparently done, we teach people they are saved but have no need to obey Jesus. This is clearly sin of not loving God and others, isn't it?

---

[24] Deuteronomy 6: 5
[25] John 14: 15

Again, we are to truly love God with everything in us. I wish we could say we could do that on our own cognitive response, but I think that we need a lot of help in this area. Watch how God shows us this in His Word as He states through John, "We love Him, because He first loved us."[26] We can only love God because He first loved us so without His power, we would be helpless to love Him. We also must understand that we wouldn't be able to love others without His power in our souls. We must be connected to God to have the ability to love another as stated "He that loveth not knoweth not God; for God is love."[27]

The American Church is supposed to be the Bride of Christ, right? God, through the writings of Paul in Ephesians, make this relationship clear as stated:

> "Husbands, love our wives, even as Christ also loved the church, and gave Himself for it; That He might sanctify and cleanse it with the washing of water by the word, That He might present it to Himself a glorious church, not having spot, or wrinkle, or any such thing; but that it should be holy and without blemish."[28]

---

[26] 1 John 4: 19
[27] 1 John 4: 8
[28] Ephesians 5: 25-27

Look at how we corporately love God in America! Are we a Bride that we can be proud of as we face the truth?

If we love God as He loves us corporately, something seems awfully wrong or out of place. God loves us with a holy and pure love and we best understand this as we study the Greek and the word for this love is called *agape* love, which is to love sacrificially and unconditionally. That is how God loves us – sacrificially and unconditionally! God tells us in the book of Matthew the words of Jesus as He stated, "37Thou shalt love the LORD thy God with all thy Heart, and with all thy soul, and with all thy mind. 38This is the first and great commandment. 39And the second is like unto it, Thou Shalt Love thy neighbor as thyself. 40On these two commandments hang all the law and the prophets."[29] Jesus tells us that we are to love God and others with the love of God, but do we see the church of America loving, or even, teaching how to love others?

I recently attended a Baptist Church in rural Arkansas not far from my home and the preacher said that "homosexuals are perverts, pedophiles, an abomination unto God and need to be saved." I leaned over to my wife and whispered, "if I was a homosexual attending this church in hopes to find the love of Christ, I would fly out of this church like my hair was on fire!" This is the fuel that gives the unbelievers the right to fight, saying that this speech on homosexual lifestyles is *"HATE SPEECH."* I agree with the secular world on this issue. We must understand that

---

[29] Matthew 22: 37 - 40

the homosexual lifestyle isn't acceptable to God and it is sin that separates a person from God. This also goes for *ALL SIN*, but we are to love that person just as when I was lost and did not know God and a person extended love to me to find Christ. The church is killing herself when she accepts that type of preaching as inspired of God. It is not! We are to hate sin and love the sinner.

We see clearly that there is a disconnect and especially when we include one of the most powerful passages of scripture on this subject as Jesus spoke these words, "34A new commandment I give unto you, that ye love one another; as I have loved you, that ye also love one another. 35By this shall all men know that ye are my disciples, if ye have love one to another."[30] We don't just need to love God because we are loved by God, but we are *COMMANDED* to love others by Jesus. Now watch this…the verse 35 states, "By this shall all men know that ye are my disciples, if ye have love one to another"[31] and I submit to you this question, do we love others as Jesus loves us, so the world knows us as His disciples? How can we do this when the church is not making disciples?

Clearly, what is killing the church of America is sin of disobedience by man. The sin of disobedience through not loving others and for not making disciples! Armed with this explanation, can we see the action of Jesus more clearly?

---

[30] John 13: 34 - 35
[31] V. 35

Chapter 3

"A Shared Path to Destruction"

"And be not conformed to this world…"
Romans 12: 2

We will see in this chapter of this book the true present condition of the American Church and the shared characteristics of the Church of Laodicea that ushered us into this death spiral. This is a very sad statement on the church, but it is one that is needed to open our eyes to the truth.

The Present Condition of the American Church

The growth of the American Church is an excellent place to begin this examination to understand the present condition. One would hope to find the American Church flourishing with a strong foundation of growth; however, the facts do not prove this out. Research reveals that there are severe problems that exist in the American Church as it is no longer experiencing growth, other than that of what is deemed "transfer growth." Ken Sidey states it this way, "Perhaps church growth's greatest challenge in North America comes from research that shows that more than 80 percent of all the growth taking place in growing churches comes through transfer, not conversion. The statistic strikes at the heart."[32] Transfer growth not only is the largest area of growth for the church, but it far outweighs any conversion growth in America. Though the decline of the church in America today is measured in numbers, the dying of the church is due to the lack of conversion growth. The church once was a growing organism and grew at an exponent rate until it went from approximately 120 people in the upper room to the state religion of the Roman Empire. The previous statement may seem oversimplified, however, not by much as Rodney Stark states, "I propose that there were a total of about a thousand Christians in the empire in the year 40."[33] Alan Hirsch reports that at a seminar the question was asked how many Christians were there before Constantine came on the scene and how many after, and the answers were as follows; "100 A.D. as few as 25,000 Christians and 310 A.D. up to 20,000,000 Christians."[34] It is obvious that the Christian community was growing strong. Allow me

---

[32] Ken Sidey, "Church Growth Fine Tunes its Formulas," <u>Christianity Today</u>, (June 24, 1991), p. 46.

[33] Rodney Stark, *The Triumph of Christianity: How the Jesus Movement Became the World's Largest Religion* (New York, NY: HarperCollins Publishers, 2011), *155*.

[34] Alan Hirsch, 2006. *The Forgotten Ways: reactivating the missional church* (Grand Rapids, MI: Baker Publishing Group), 18.

to do the math on this issue. If Stark is correct and there were 20,000,000 Christians developed in 310 years, that would break down to be 64,516 *new* Christians each year for 310 years. That is amazingly staggering isn't it, that many new Christians for over 300 years? Now, compare that number to the present-day church in America. Do we have 64, 516 new converts to Christ in *ANY YEAR*? I think not. Stark also stated, "And it is generally agreed that by the year 350, Christians were in the majority – if barely – amounting to somewhat more than 30 million who were at least nominal Christians."[35] As one looks to the historical data of Christianity, the growth was predominantly achieved by conversion. Again, Stark's opinion on the matter of conversion is:

> "Conversion is primarily about bringing one's religious behavior into alignment with that of one's friends and relatives, not about encountering attractive doctrines. Put more formally: people tend to convert to a religious group when their social ties to members outweigh their ties to outsiders who might oppose the conversion, and this often occurs before a convert knows much about what the group believes."[36]

---

[35] Stark, *The Triumph of Christianity*, 156.
[36] Stark, *The Triumph of Christianity*, 68.

The correlation of the previous statements and data can be that if the majority of the American Churches are either plateauing (flat lined) or in decline, the church cannot be experiencing conversion growth. The church must learn or re-learn how to express the salvation story and reach out to others or the church will die. Benton Johnson, Dean Hoge, and Donald Luidens make their case on this subject as they explain:

> "The underlying problem of the mainline churches cannot be solved by new programs of church development alone. That problem is the weakening of the spiritual conviction required to generate the enthusiasm and energy needed to sustain a vigorous communal life. Somehow, in the course of the past century, these churches lost the will or the ability to teach the Christian faith."[37]

Obviously, the church is losing ground and the numbers are staggering due to the lack of passion and commitment to the teaching of the Christian faith which begins and ends with the person of Jesus Christ. This is a major reason why, not only is the church in decline numerically, but it is slowly dying because of the lack of desire to make disciples for Jesus Christ. Barna

---

[37] Benton Johnson, Dean R Hoge and Donald A Luidens, "Mainline Churches: The Real Reason for Decline." First Things 31, (March 1993): 13-18. ATLA Religion Database with ATLASerials, EBSCOhost (accessed July 5, 2016).

adds, "Since 1980, there has been 'no growth' in the proportion of the adult population that can be classified as 'born again' Christians. The proportion of born-again Christians has remained constant at 32% despite the fact that churches and para-church organizations have spent billions of dollars on evangelism. More than 10,000 hours of evangelistic television programming have been broadcast, in excess of 5,000 new Christian books have been published, and more than 1,000 radio stations carry Christian programming. Yet despite such widespread opportunities for exposure to the Gospel, there has been no discernable growth in the size of the Christian body."[38] That is an amazing fact that seems bone chilling and reveals much about the Church of America.

I have had the privilege to visit and attempt to work with churches on this issue of evangelization of their community. To make an impact statement to their church I would begin with this statement, "If your church closed today, would this community notice or even care?" The people of this church may care but what about the community at large? Sadly, most churches could close today, and no one would care. The main reason is that the church isn't in the business of penetrating the community for Jesus Christ. Allow me to unpack that statement for you. If a church (body of Christ) is not in the business of sharing the truth about Jesus to the community, they probably are experiencing one of two problems, or both.

---

[38] Barna, *Marketing the Church*, 26.

The first problem may be that the leader of the church does not understand the need or the methods necessary to accomplish this task, so he doesn't make it essential to the congregation and therefore, the church doesn't go in a systematic and organized methodology to penetrate the community. This could be simple lack of knowledge and understanding. The second problem is the one I explained previously; the church simply doesn't love others because Christ isn't in them so they can't offer it to others. There is a great and powerful line from the movie "Fireproof." The son is expressing great frustration about his wife and he is about done trying to make the marriage work and the father offers him some great advice. He tells his son that his wife is wanting to be loved and the truth is that his son can't offer what he doesn't have. The father has moved physically under the cross as he explains this to his son, and it makes for a powerful lesson for us all. Do you have what it takes to love others? John teaches us in the Bible, "Beloved, let us love one another: for love is of God; and everyone that loveth is born of God, and knoweth God. He that loveth not knoweth not God: for God is love."[39] This statement is a little clearer in another version of the Bible as it states, "Dear friends, let us love one another, for love comes from God. Everyone who loves has been born of God and knows God. Whoever does not love does not know God, because God is love."[40] The love we need isn't

---

[39] 1 John 4: 7-8
[40] 1 John 4: 7-8 (NIV)

a worldly love, but a love birthed in God. If you are not connected to God through Christ Jesus, then you cannot love another.

Another revealing fact that the Church of America is in decline, and slowly dying, is offered by Carlson and Lueken as they state, "Every year more than 4,000 churches close their doors compared to approximately 1,000 new (and mostly very small) churches that start."[41] This statistic must break the heart of any and all Christians as the doors of approximately 4,000 churches close each year. That is 4,000 congregations that no longer worship together, pray together, fellowship together and the darkness fills the buildings that once heard the praises of God. Kent Carlson and Mike Lueken also note that "half of all churches in the U.S. did not add any new members to their ranks between 2010 and 2012."[42] An incredible statistic as over half of the Churches of America did not add one new member to the ranks in those years. This would mean that very few, if any, new converts of Jesus Christ were able to reject the darkness and come to the light for salvation. If those who did somehow receive conversion, they must not have been included in the rolls of the church for discipleship either.

People who go to church, and call themselves Christians, have serious issues understanding, and

---

[41] Kent Carlson and Mike Lueken, *Renovation of the Church* (Downers Grove, IL: InterVarsity Press, 2011), 40.
[42] Ibid. 76–77.

accepting Christianity today, which may be a reason for the decline in the church. According to Barna only six out of ten Christians believe the Bible is totally accurate in all its teachings,[43] which leaves four out of ten Christians that doubt the Word of God. Many Christians believe that Jesus was not sinless during His time on earth as thirty-seven percent believe that Jesus did commit sins.[44] Also, Barna's research data shows that many Christians do not believe in the person of the Holy Spirit but only think of Him as a symbol as sixty-two percent of Christians believe this.[45] This is a major reason, that if Christians do not believe in the inerrancy of the Bible, the sinlessness of Jesus Christ, and the person of the Holy Spirit, why they are no long attending a church that promotes this view, causing the slow death of the church. The problem stated clearly as Jonathan Falwell gives a simple understanding for solution as he says, "Church growth is really more of a matter of growing and developing disciples. The body will grow in quantity as it also intentionally develops each individual to reach their full potential in Christ."[46]

---

[43] Barna, *Growing True Disciples,* 65.

[44] Barna, *Growing True Disciples,* 65.

[45] Barna, *Growing True Disciples,* 65.

[46] Jonathan Falwell, Gen. Ed. *Innovatechurch: innovative leadership for the next generation church* (Nashville, TN: B&H Publishing Group, 2008), 111.

Shared Characteristics of the church of Laodicea and the Church of America

The church of Laodicea has several characteristics that are amazingly like the characteristics of the Worldly church and/or the Church of America in the modern era. A major characteristic can be found in the lukewarmness that was found in the church of Laodicea. Is this a characteristic of the Church of America? According to Hal Lindsey it is, as he states, "Although this Laodicean lukewarmness is the predominant characteristic of the church age today, there are signs that the Philadelphian evangelistic fervor is reviving in these closing days of human history. That's consistent with God's pattern of always showering down grace before hurling blasts of judgment."[47] He does confirm that a judgment is coming on the modern day American Church which is the "spewing out" that Jesus spoke of, but interestingly he believes that there will be an evangelistic movement prior to the Great Tribulation. At this point, though I believe that Jesus has spewed out the American Church, I am not looking for the outpouring of the Holy Spirit until we begin the reformation process and come into the Will of God as His church. I want to offer this as a possibility on the outpouring of the Holy Spirit. Either God *will* send the outpouring of the Holy Spirit once the American Church reforms or He has

---

[47] Hal Lindsey, *There's A New World Coming: A Prophetic Odyssey* (Santa Ana, CA: Vision House Publishers, 1973), 72.

already sent this outpouring in the 1800's in the Great Revivals of that time. This could be a truth, but I am not stating this as one, only that it could be a possibility of one truth.

One thing for sure is what David Graves has said, "Our passion for Christ ought to lead to a healing (hot) for the spiritually sick, and refreshment (cold) for the spiritually weary. Our service for Christ should flow with fresh water of service and not a lukewarm apathy for the needs of others. Christ prefers us either hot or cold, but lukewarm behavior makes Him want to vomit."[48] The word apathy means to have a lack of emotion, feeling or interest in a person or thing. Apathy breeds lukewarmness as the Christians of today, as well as yesteryear, are empty and emotionless as it comes to a relationship with God and His mission. K. H. Brooks states, "The lack of overall health in the church at this particular time is due in part to the failure of the church to practice biblical discipleship and accountability. The apathy which exists in the church is evident not only in the members of the average church body but also among the staff including the pastor."[49] If they are apathetic toward God, they will not take to heart the relationship nor the call to serve God in accordance with His Word.

---

[48] David E. Graves, "Jesus Speaks to Seven of His Churches, Part 2." Journal – Bible and Spade (Second Run) – Volume – BSPADE 23: 3 (Summer, 2010). 9.

[49] K. H. Brooks, (2014). *Addressing apathy in the church: Moving people towards a biblical healthy discipleship model* (Order No. 3636361). Available from Dissertations & Theses @ Liberty University. 1.

May I state that I thought about naming this book "A Den of Thieves." We see in the Bible, "And said unto them, it is written, My house shall be called the house of Prayer, but ye have made it a den of thieves." [50] This passage of scripture in the Bible is called the cleansing of the temple. Is that what the American Church needs today? Our apathy toward God as a church (body of Christ) is the reason for the spewing out of the church. If we think about this closely, the people in the temple at the time of Christ were people who only cared for themselves and trying to profit from others. Can you feel the "righteous anger" that Jesus explodes with and to these people? Look at what they have done to God's House. Could Jesus be exploding with His anger today over how we have destroyed God's House of Prayer and turned it into a Den of Thieves. Another place in the Bible we find Jesus having "righteous anger," I believe, is in Mark where Jesus has healed a leper "And he straitly charged him, and forthwith sent him away."[51] The word "straitly" means strictly and this gives the indication that Jesus was harsh to him out of righteous anger. There could be a number of different reasons, but suffice to say, Jesus was righteously angered. If we are not in a true relationship with God, if we are not in obedience to God's commandments, if we are only seeking to please ourselves, are we not the same as those who turned God's

---

[50] Matthew 21: 13
[51] Mark 1: 43

house of prayer into a den of thieves? If we haven't been spewed out of the bowels of Jesus, we can at least see and understand how angered He must be with us.

In the Church of America, it is apparent that many church members don't even care enough to invite others to join them in church services. Rainer makes an interesting point as he says, "Only 21 percent of active churchgoers invite anyone to church in the course of a year. But only 2 percent of church members invite an unchurched person to church. Perhaps the evangelistic apathy so evident in many of our churches can be explained by simple laziness on the part of church members in inviting others to church."[52] The words of Jesus on the subject of service must be falling on deaf ears in many of the modern churches as they did on the historical church. Jesus says, "If any man serve me, let him follow me; and where I am, there shall also my servant be: if any man serve me, him will my Father honour."[53] If one doesn't care about the Word of God and this relationship with God to serve others, this is a reason for the dying of the church. According to Barna, "How can you and your faith community serve the unchurched, motivated by nothing but love? The goal is to serve the churchless, not because it proves our spiritual self-worth, but because it's the Jesus thing to do."[54]

---

[52] Rainer, *The Unchurched Next Door*, 25.

[53] John 12:26.

[54] Barna and Kinnaman, *Churchless*, 186.

The second characteristic of the church of Laodicea shared with the Church of America can be found in the area of disobedience to God. The sin of disobedience that is apparent in the church of Laodicea and the American Church is one of self-sufficiency. The sin of self-centeredness leads one to think they are in the center and that they must take care of their needs and this leads man to self-sufficiency. However, the Bible reveals a different plan for man. Jesus begins and shows the church that, what they believe is truly opposite from the truth. Jesus tells the angel of the church of Laodicea, "Because thou sayest, I am rich, and increased with good, and have need of nothing; and knowest not that thou art wretched, and miserable, and poor, and blind, and naked."[55] Jesus is saying the exact words to the Church of America as she stands in her obstinacy to God by her reliance on her riches and self-sufficiency due to self-centeredness. In the eyes of God, the church of Laodicea was in horrible shape as they were wretched, miserable, poor, blind, and naked, but to the church of Laodicea, they saw themselves as rich in money, self-sufficient, and in no need of Jesus Christ. How blind is the Church of America as she refuses to see herself in the same sin? This sin is that of self-centeredness and a rejection of the reliance on God and a need to remain self-sufficient for their own pleasures and desires. According to Millard Erickson, "We need to look more closely at the human sin of self-centeredness. The essence

---

[55] Revelation 3:17.

of the sin does not lie in preferring ourselves to others, but in preferring some finite thing to the supreme value, God."[56] Though both churches held to their position of self-centeredness and self-sufficiency, God in his Word shows man he needs to be dependent on God. The entire passage of Psalm 86 shows both churches their true need – the need to obey and trust God and remain reliant on Him. Man has great need to be dependent upon God for everything from life, breath, love, forgiveness, and sustenance in all. A powerful Scripture found in Psalm 86 is one that illuminates the position of David which is diametrically opposed to both churches as he states, "Bow down thine ear, O Lord, hear me: for I am poor and needy."[57] In humility, David admits he is poor and needy where both churches feel they are rich and in need of nothing. Another Scripture that illuminates man's need for reliance on God is found in the book of Proverbs, "Trust in the Lord with all thine heart; and lean not unto thine own understanding."[58] Both of these Scriptures are found in the Old Testament and would have been accessible to the church of Laodicea but in their sin, they rejected the reliance on God and traded it for their own self-centeredness and self-sufficiency. Could this truly be an issue of idol worship? If both churches are self-centered and self-reliant it appears that the bigger issue is that

---

[56] Millard J. Erickson, *Christian Theology.* 2nd ed.(Grand Rapids, MI: Baker Academic, 1998), 314.

[57] Psalm 86:1.

[58] Proverbs 3:5.

"self" is the god and both churches have turned away from the true God. Through Moses, God spoke these words, "I am the Lord thy God, which have brought thee out of the land of Egypt, out of the house of bondage. Thou shalt have no other gods before me."[59] It appears that both churches have gods before the true God, and this is idol worship. Though idolatry is as old as man himself, the Bible speaks at great length against idolatry. Elwell speaks clearly on this subject as he states:

> "In the later history of Christianity, idolatry in the strict sense has continued to be opposed in the terms of the ancient biblical prohibitions. But the continuing danger has more commonly returned in the metaphorical sense delineated in the NT; it is the "worship" (i.e., the total dedication of a person) of that which is seen and tangible, the goals of covetousness, rather than the unseen spiritual being that is God."[60]

The third characteristic of the church of Laodicea is found in the area of compromise. The Word of God found in Joshua says:

> "Now therefore fear the Lord and serve him in sincerity and in truth: and put away the

---

[59] Exodus 20:2–3.
[60] Elwell, *Evangelical Dictionary of Theology*, 589.

gods which your fathers served on the other side of the flood, and in Egypt; and serve ye the Lord. And if it seems evil unto you to serve the Lord, choose you this whom ye will serve; whether the gods which your fathers served that were on the other side of the flood, or the gods of the Amorites, in whose land ye dwell: but as for me and my house, we will serve the Lord."[61]

To serve the Lord God Almighty, one must first surrender his will, bow, and obey the will of God. One must not compromise the Word of God but simply obey. This is a difficult concept for many in their walk with Jesus Christ. As the God of Self is the God of both churches, is it easier to understand that man won't bend his knee to the true God. One day all knees will bend and all men will bow before Him, "For it is written, 'As I live', saith the Lord, 'every knee shall bow to me, and every tongue shall confess to God.'"[62] This may be a major reason for the dying of the church as man and his desire to please his god, Self, and exchange the truth for a lie. In God's word, He states, "Who changed the truth of God into a lie and worshipped and served the creature more than the Creator, who is blessed forever. Amen."[63]

---

[61] Joshua 24:14–15.
[62] Romans 14:11.
[63] Romans 1:25.

Obliviously, man is off the path of righteousness and on a path of destruction and this is very similar to the church of Laodicea. A major characteristic is both churches are in sin. James teaches this as he said, "Therefore to him that knoweth to do good, and doeth it not, to him it is sin."[64]

The fourth characteristic that is similar, appears to be the bowing of the church and her leaders, to the people, or congregants, and their desires and demands instead of the lifting up and the worship in obedience to the name of Jesus Christ. The church of Laodicea was completely self-sufficient and in need of nothing including the presence of Jesus Christ in their church and the worldly church appears to be self-sufficient with no need for the presence of Jesus Christ in their church. The worldly American Church seems to follow the need of the people and their desires and their rights much more than the need to obey and follow the commandments of God.

Pastors of today that have accepted leadership positions in Churches of America have a tremendous responsibility and must know they are first called by God for service as well as have the courage to take a stand and lead their flock in accordance with God's Word. According to Scazzero, "The overall health of any church or ministry depends primarily on the emotional and spiritual health of its leadership. In fact, the key to successful spiritual leadership has much more to do with the leader's internal

---

[64] James 4:17.

life than with the leader's expertise, gifts, or experience."[65]
John MacArthur states this quite eloquently as he says:

> "In the ministry, pressure to compromise, to
> mitigate the message, and to avoid offending
> sinners will always exist. However, the
> preacher's job is to expose sin, to confront the
> lost with the hopelessness of their condition,
> and to offer the cure for their wretchedness
> in the saving gospel of Jesus Christ. Doing
> those things will lead to confrontation
> and opposition. The courage to stand firm
> derives from a humble dependence on God's
> power."[66]

If a pastor is a true called man of God, he will stand
against this type of pressure and trust God to deliver
him either through an acceptance of God's truth by
the congregation or a removal by God's hand from that
church. A truly called man of God will stand before
God and will be completely dependent upon His power
and not the approval of those who pay him money.
MacArthur continues on this point as he states, "A man of
God must flee the evils associated with the love of money:
various temptations, snares, harmful desires which lead to

---

[65] Scazzero, Peter. 2010. *The Emotionally Healthy Church: A Strategy for Discipleship that Actually Changes Lives.* Grand Rapids, MI: Zondervan. 20.

[66] John MacArthur, *Pastoral Ministry: How to Shepherd Biblically* (Nashville, TN: Thomas Nelson, Inc., 2005), 18.

destruction, apostasy, and sorrow. Greed is the enemy. It will destroy the man of God, so he must run from it."[67] As it is stated by God through Paul in Ephesians 6:10, "Finally, my brethren, be strong in the Lord, and in the power of his might." God desires to call a man as His pastor for His church. Jeremiah 3:15, "And I will give you pastors according to mine heart, which shall feed you with knowledge and understanding." According to Charles Spurgeon:

> "Now, all in a church cannot oversee, or rule – there must be some to be overseen and ruled; and we believe that the Holy Ghost appoints in the church of God some to act as overseers, while others are made willing to be watched over for their good. All are not called to labour in word and doctrine, or to be elders, or to exercise the office of a bishop; nor should all aspire to such works, since the gifts necessary are nowhere promised to all; but those should addict themselves to such important engagements who feel, like the apostle, that they have received this ministry."[68]

---

[67] John MacArthur, *Preaching: How to Preach Biblically* (Nashville, TN: Thomas Nelson, Inc., 2005), 64.

[68] Charles Spurgeon, *Lectures to My Students: Complete and Unabridged* (Grand Rapids, MI: Zondervan, 1954), 22.

However, it is noted in the Word of God found in Jeremiah that a man should not serve God in this capacity if he is not called by God. Jeremiah 23:32, "Behold, I am against them that prophesy false dreams, saith the Lord, and do tell them, and cause my people to err by their lies, and by their lightness; yet I sent them not, nor commanded them: therefore, they shall not profit this people at all, saith the Lord." God is against any man who is not called by God and teaches false doctrine and lies to His people under the "calling" of God that truly he has not received. A pastor who is not called by God, but a career pastor will succumb to the pressure and only preach what seems appropriate to that congregation. This is another reason that the Church in America is dying due to compromise and greed.

The sad state of affairs in the American Church is that many pastors are not truly called by God and many of those who are called by God are not standing strong in His power to lead their flocks according to the Word of God. Could the Scripture of Paul found in 2 Timothy that says, "Having a form of godliness, but denying the power thereof from such turn away" still hold truth to man as he should recognize the fact the church only has a form of godliness but denies the power of God and he should turn away?[69] Graves also states clearly:

---

[69] 2 Timothy 3:5.

"Throughout history there have been churches like these seven churches. The call extends to the Church today to hear the voice of the Spirit in a culture that summons the Church to compromise. The Church still struggles with formalism, idolatry, materialism, apathy, lack of love, persecution, and false teachers. As the Church awaits the Lord's return, it must watch (Mt 24:52; Mk 13:35) and pray to be faithful to the Savior."[70]

The Church of America is in a desperate place in history and in the path of God's judgment if something is not done soon. Willmington adds, "The church age: Little comment is needed to describe the sad state of Christendom as it exists today. Many groups which brazenly carry the name of Christian seem to prefer Communism to democracy, encourage immorality, support anarchy, downplay every important biblical doctrine, and ridicule Bible believers."[71]

---

[70] Graves, "Jesus Speaks to Seven of His Churches, Part 2," 9.
[71] Harold L. Wilmington. *Willmington's Guide to the Bible. Vol. 2 New Testament.* Wheaton, IL: Tyndale House Publishers. 1986. 286.

Chapter 4

"God's Rejection of His Church"

"So then because thou art lukewarm,
and neither cold nor hot,
I will spue thee out of my mouth"
Revelation 3: 16

Jesus's Action to the American Church: Rejection

I am going to make a statement that will shock you. Are you ready? I believe that Jesus has spit out the American Church! *OUCH*! Allow me to explain. God spoke through John as he wrote the book of Revelation and we see the words of Jesus to His churches, "So then because thou art lukewarm, and neither cold nor hot, I will spue thee out of my mouth."[72] He was speaking to the church of Laodicea and the American Church. He did spit out the church of Laodicea and I believe that He has spit out the Church of America. Most of us are taught

---

[72] Revelation 3: 16

that the book of Revelation is a futuristic book. At some point, the future that the book of Revelation speaks of becomes the present. I believe that is today! Allow me to examine this subject with you. It is my belief that we must have a complete understanding of this subject so we can grasp the full truth. We must examine this issue from the historical truth about the Church of Laodicea and from the prophetic eyes of Jesus.

The Historical Church of Laodicea

The church of Laodicea existed historically and was in the city of Laodicea located approximately ninety miles due east of Ephesus and approximately fifty miles southeast of the city of Philadelphia in Asia Minor. R. L. Overstreet states this data this way, "The seventh city on the circuitous Roman road in Asia Minor was Laodicea, about sixty miles southeast of Philadelphia and about one hundred miles east of Ephesus."[73]

The city of Laodicea was built on an earlier site called Diospolis which meant City of Zeus. This city also laid claims to the deity of Zeus and a temple was constructed to Zeus. However, Mitchell Reddish makes it very clear on the origin of the city of Laodicea as he states, "Laodicea was established in the middle of the third century BC by the Seleucid king, Antiochus II, who named the city

---

[73] R. L. Overstreet, *The Temple of God in the Book of Revelation. Bibliotheca Sacra* 166, no. 664 (2009): 446-462.

after his wife Laodice (whom he divorced soon after)."[74] The two historic cities that are mentioned in the Bible, but not in the book of Revelation by name, that were the closest to Laodicea were the cities of Colossae, and Hierapolis. The city, as well as the church, of Laodicea was a very wealthy city. In the city of Laodicea, three major resources contributed to the wealth; a banking center, a large manufacturing center, and a large medical school. The medical school was famous and contributed to the overall wealth of the city and the church. George Ladd cites an important point as it relates to the school, as he says, "Laodicea was also the seat of a flourishing medical school which was particularly noted for its ear ointment and for "Phrygian powder" which was used in the manufacture of eye-salve."[75] Reddish confirms the previous statement but also adds a major point concerning the wealth of the city as he states, "Laodicea was famous for its banking industry, its textile production, and its medical school....During the first century A.D., the city was economically prosperous. When an earthquake destroyed the city in A.D. 60, the city refused imperial assistance, instead opting to rebuild the city out of its own financial resources."[76] The city of Laodicea was situated near the banks of the Lycus River in the valley near

---

[74] Mitchell G. Reddish, *Smyth & Helwys Bible Commentary: Revelation* (Macon, GA: Smyth & Helwys Publishing, Inc. 2001), 79.

[75] George Eldon Ladd, *A Commentary on the Revelation of John* (Grand Rapids, MI: Wm. B. Eerdmans Publishing Co., 1972), 64.

[76] Reddish, *Smyth & Helwys Bible Commentary: Revelation,* 79.

Colossae and Hierapolis. All three churches are supported by the Scriptures found in the book of Colossians, "To the saints and faithful brethren in Christ which are at Colossae:...."[77] and also Paul says, "For I bear him record, that he hath a great zeal for you, and them that are in Laodicea, and them in Hierapolis."[78] The city of Laodicea was located at the junction of three great roads that traversed Asia Minor.

One of the major areas for the city that presented itself as problematic was that in the condition of the city's water supply. Historically, the city of Colossae, located approximately ten miles southeast of Laodicea, was known for its pure cold water supply, however, on the opposite side of the coin, the city of Hierapolis, located approximately five to six miles from Laodicea, was also known for its water but it was because of the medicinal qualities found in the hot waters of the city. The city of Laodicea had to receive its water through the aqueduct system from the city of Colossae and by the time the water was delivered it was not only lukewarm, but it was the cause of illness from bacteria. John McRay has an interesting take on this subject as he believes that the sickness that the Laodiceans suffered was from the waters being bathed in prior to being sent through the aqueduct to Laodicea. John McRay states:

---

[77] Colossians 1:2
[78] Colossians 4:13.

"White mineral deposits collected over millennia around putrid warm springs at this resort town. Perhaps the sensuality of bathing in the spring waters infected residents of neighboring Laodicea and prompted the graphic warning of Revelation 3:16: to declare of the city's conduct, "because you are lukewarm, and neither cold nor hot, I will vomit you out of my mouth" (author's translation). Water piped into Laodicea by aqueduct from the south was so concentrated with minerals that the Roman engineers designed vents, capped by removable stones, so the aqueduct pipes could periodically be cleared of deposits."[79]

The earthquake devastated the entire region of the Lycus River Valley and there is evidence that the cities of Laodicea, Colossae, and Hierapolis were heavily damaged. However due to the wealth and resources found in the city of Laodicea, she was able to rebuild and again prosper without any help from others.

The church of Laodicea was the benefactor of the great wealth found in the city of Laodicea and was in need of nothing as Jesus states in the Scriptures of Revelation 3:17, "Because thou sayest, I am rich, and increased with

---

[79] John McRay, *Archaeology & The New Testament* (Grand Rapids, MI: Baker House Company, 1997), 248.

goods, and have need of nothing…" According to D. Guthrie and J. A. Motyer:

> "The claim of the Laodiceans is not merely that they need nothing, but that their wealth, moral as well as material, is entirely due to their own efforts. Their real condition is shown to be one of poverty, in spite of their money; nakedness, despite their abundance of cloth; blindness, though they have many physicians. This church, therefore, alone of all the seven, is called 'the pitiable one.'"[80]

Jesus then tells them in Revelation 3:19, "As many as I love, I rebuke and chasten: be zealous therefore, and repent."[81] Jesus states He loves them and though His words have been difficult to hear, He confirms that He does love them and they need to repent of their sins against God. William Barclay has an interesting take on this subject as he says:

> "Let us first take the word *rebuke*. The Greek is *elegchein* and it describes the kind of rebuke which compels a man to see the error of his ways. The rebuke of God is not so much punishment as illumination…. The

---

[80] D. Guthrie, ed. and J. A. Motyer, ed., *New Bible Commentary*. 3rd ed (Carmel, NY: B. Eerdmans Publishing Company, 1970), 1287.
[81] Revelation 3:19

discipline of God is not something which we should resent, but something for which we should be devoutly thankful."[82]

Jesus is saying how much He loves them but due to their sin He will rebuke them and prior to any punishment, Jesus wants them to understand why they will receive chastisement. However, there is no indication recorded that the historical church of Laodicea ever truly saw their sin and no recorded documentation that this church ever repented from her sin against God. Therefore, there is much support for the fact that Laodicea was a real church that existed in a real city of history in Asia Minor.

The Prophetic Church of Laodicea

I believe we now must turn the attention to the prophetic understanding of the discussion of the seven churches in Revelation with a focus on the church of Laodicea. The book of Revelation was written by the apostle John at approximately A.D. 95 – 100 and would be historically correct to understand that there were many established churches around the time of the writing of the book of Revelation. Of those churches, it is apparent that Paul birthed many of them and of those he did not give birth, he was certainly a heavy influence on those who began a church. Jesus Christ selected only seven of these

---

[82] William Barclay, *The Revelation of John, Volume 1 (Chapters 1 to 5).* Revised Ed. (Philadelphia, PA: The Westminster Press, 1976), 145 – 146.

churches to address through the apostle John in the book of Revelation.

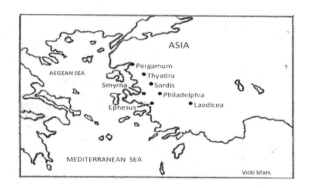

Clearly, the message from Jesus was directed literally to those seven historical churches and it is also clearly, the same messages to these churches could be applicable to all churches in every age. However, Harold Willmington has an interesting take on this subject as he states the following:

> "The chronological purpose: that the characteristics of these churches serve as a prophetical preview of the seven great periods in Christendom from Pentecost to the rapture. A suggested outline of this predictive panorama may be seen as follows:
>
> 1. Ephesus (A.D. 30 – 300) – name means "desirable." The Apostolic Church.
> 2. Smyrna (100 – 313) – name means "myrrh." The Martyr Church.

3. Pergamos (314 – 590) – name means marriage." The Compromising Church.

4. Thyatira (590 – 1517) – name means "continual sacrifice." The Roman Catholic Church.

5. Sardis (1517 – 1700) – name means "remnant." The Reformation Church.

6. Philadelphia (1700 – 1900) – name means "brotherly love." The Revival Church.

7. Laodicea (1900 – rapture) – name means "people's rights." The Worldly Church."[83]

The worldly church is a name that should strike fear in all true believers of Jesus Christ as it resonates with the correlation of the true church of Jesus Christ becoming the compromised church of the world. The name Laodicea has been interpreted to mean a variety of different meanings. According to Jerry Falwell:

> "The church at Laodicea (rights of the people) is the church of insipid lukewarmness. It describes the moral condition of the church at the close of the church age. The people demand their rights with democracy and almost anarchy as the result."[84]

Could this also be connected to the reasons that Paul

---

[83] Willmington, *Willmington's Guide to the Bible: Vol. 2 New Testament*, 278.

[84] Jerry D. Falwell, ed., *Liberty Bible Commentary: The Old-time Gospel Hour Edition* (Nashville, TN: Thomas Nelson, Inc., 1983), 2666.

spoke to Timothy as in the Scripture that states, "For the time will come when they will not endure sound doctrine; but after their own lusts shall they heap to themselves teachers, having itching ears;"[85]

Jesus informs the church that due to their lukewarmness He will "spew" them out.[86] The people of the church of Laodicea were not hot or cold for Jesus but only lukewarm. Martin Kiddle paints this picture as he states, "For better to be completely untouched by the flame of religion than to have only smouldering embers, half choked in ashes."[87]

Jesus gives an invitation and a promise to the church of Laodicea as He states:

> "Behold, I stand at the door, and knock: if any man hears my voice, and open the door, I will come in to him, and will sup with him, and he with me. To him that overcometh will I grant to sit with me in my throne, even as I also overcame and am set down with my Father in his throne. He that hath an ear, let him hear what the Spirit saith unto the churches."[88]

Jesus is clearly telling the church of Laodicea that they

---

[85] 2 Timothy 4:3.
[86] Revelation 3:16.
[87] Martin Kiddle and M. K. Ross, *The Revelation of St. John* (New York, NY: Harper & Brothers Publishers, 1941), 58.
[88] Revelation 3:20–22.

need to repent and return to God. If they do this, they will receive this invitation and promise. Reddish states, "Although often understood in individualistic terms, this promise is perhaps best understood as a corporate promise addressed to the church."[89] Jesus says He is at the door and knocking so man will invite him into His church. If man chooses to refuse to allow Christ into His Church, there is a warning of judgement. According to the views of John Walvoord as he states:

> "Having concluded the messages to the seven churches culminating in the message to the church at Laodicea, the invitation becomes a personal one to all who will hear the words of warning. The prophetic foreshadowing provided in the seven churches as representative of churches found throughout the entire history of the church as special application in connection with the church at Laodicea. Under this point of view the state of this church is typical of the church of the last days and is therefore an exhortation to self-judgment and dedication to the will of God especially appropriate for the consideration in modern days."[90]

---

[89] Reddish, *Revelation*, 83.
[90] John Walvoord, *The Revelation of Jesus Christ: A Commentary By John F. Walvoord* (Chicago, IL: Moody Press, 1966), 97.

Walvoord also states, "The final message to the church at Laodicea is the crowning indictment, a warning against the danger of lukewarmness (3:15–16), of self-sufficiency, of being unconscious of desperate spiritual need. To contemporary churches each of these messages is amazingly relevant and pointed in its searching analysis of what our Lord sees as he stands in the midst of the lampstands."[91] A warning of judgement of God on the church as God will take His hand off the church and usher in the seven year period called the Tribulation which follows the rapture of the church. According to Barclay, "It is in fact, God's final punishment to leave a man alone. "Ephraim is joined to idols; let him alone. (Hosea 4:17).""[92]

Jesus says to him that overcometh, and man can overcometh his sin with the repentance which is the turning away from and then the turning to God for forgiveness of his sins. If man can do this, he then will sit with Jesus at the right hand of the Father, but if he chooses not to repent, the future doesn't look so bright. This Scripture was given to the church of Laodicea as well as the other churches and this ties this church especially

---

[91] Walvoord, *The Revelation of Jesus Christ*, 100.
[92] Barclay, *The Revelation of John*, 145.

to the prophetic, as this message wasn't simply given to this church but to all man and churches of the future. According to Barclay:

> "It generalizes the message of the letter. It means that their message was not confined to the people in the seven churches nineteen hundred years ago, but that through them the Spirit is speaking to every man in every generation. We have set these letters carefully against the local situations to which they were addressed; but their message is not local and temporary. It is eternal and in them the Spirit still speaks to us."[93]

It is important to look at the big picture and understand that Jesus is speaking to all generations and not simply one localized body.

There is a definite correlation of the facts and truths concerning the church of Laodicea and the Church of America. Merrill Tenney makes a strong comment on this subject as he states:

> "The letters to the seven churches close the section of Revelation that relates to the immediate present of the author. To what extent they forecast the development of

---

[93] Barclay, *The Revelation of John*, 149.

the historic church may be debatable. The probability that they have a meaning for the church of all time is enhanced by one prominent fact: the increasing imminence of the Lord's coming is reflected in His utterances of correction to these churches..."[94]

Though this may be debatable, there is a strong probability that the letters are speaking to future generations and not simply to a local church of that time.

---

[94] Merrill C. Tenney, *Interpreting Revelation* (Grand Rapids, MI: Wm. B. Eerdmans Publishing Company, 1957), 68.

Chapter 5

Learning from History

"For whatsoever things were written aforetime were written for our learning, that we through patience and comfort of the scriptures might have hope."
Romans 15: 4

The History of Discipleship and Small Groups

Discipleship is the key to victory for the Church of America and for the glory of God. I believe that it has been established that the American Church has lost her way. She no longer shows, teaches, or extends love to the world as she refuses to make disciples of Jesus Christ and just as important, she refuses to make leaders of disciples of Jesus Christ. I believe that is important for you, the reader, to grasp a thorough understanding of the history of discipleship to understand the depth that we have fallen. I hope this chapter will give you a deeper understanding of the great need to return to obeying the commandments of Jesus Christ and begin to make disciples and show the love of Jesus to the world!

Discipleship is a complex process that consists of many different elements and is best facilitated Biblically through the small group format. According to Hull, "discipleship means the state of being a disciple. In fact, the term discipleship has a nice ongoing feel – a sense of journey, the idea of becoming a disciple rather than having been made a disciple."[95] It is important to gain a clear and concise understanding of the whole picture of discipleship as progressed through the years. Also, a short historical look into the history of small groups will give an understanding of how they have been utilized over the years.

Discipleship

In the following examination of the facts, it is imperative that one understands that there needs to be a clear definition and explanation of terms. As one examines the history of discipleship, it will be abundantly clear that even in the first century, and every century that followed, there was a deep understanding for the need for discipleship. Also, included in the long history of discipleship, one will find that there are many different methods and models in which to disciple others. Zempel states, "I would say that there are as many ways to do

---

[95] Hull, Bill. *The Complete Book Of Discipleship: On Being And Making Followers Of Christ.* Colorado Springs, CO: NavPress. 2006. 35.

discipleship as there are people. C. S. Lewis said, "Let God be as unique with others as he was with you." That means there are billions of ways to do discipleship."[96] In this project, the review of the many different methods of discipleship will not be possible but there will be a review of a number of the major methods most commonly utilized.

Discipleship cannot occur without disciples, so a strong definition of the word disciple would be needed at this point. According to Early and Dempsey, "A disciple is a person who has trusted Christ for salvation and has surrendered completely to Him. He or she is committed to practicing the spiritual disciplines in community and developing to their full potential for Christ and His mission."[97] Though there are many definitions of this word today, I would say that this is possibly the most comprehensive of all definitions. Jesus is the foundation on which one would look to as the best example of our disciple maker. So once a person becomes a disciple of Jesus, he would simply look to the process that Jesus used to make disciples and go forth to multiply, in Christ, that effort. Disciples then begin the process of making other disciples, creating leaders to make more disciples, and this would be the process of discipleship. A strong definition

---

[96] Zempel, Heather. *Models of Discipleship Throughout Church History.* http://discipleshipgroups.blogspot.com/2006/02/models-of-discipleship-throughout.html. 2006. 1.

[97] Earley and Dempsey. *Disciple Making Is...: How to Live the Great Commission with Passion and Confidence.* 28.

of the word discipleship can be found in the writings of Dempsey, as he states, "Discipleship is the process of guiding individual disciples to grow in spiritual maturity and to discover and use their gifts, talents and abilities in fulfillment of Christ's mission."[98]

An examination of the history of the Christian discipleship process will be discussed, as well as, is this still an appropriate plan for the church of the present day? This writing will look at the history of discipleship using the Biblical foundations, discipleship in the Gospels, the book of Acts, the Epistles, and down through the centuries. Also, a close look at the vehicle that was chosen to drive this process which was the small group format.

One of the most important themes that seem to be woven into the fabric of the history of Christian discipleship is that of "community." In each of the following areas of examination, one will find that community is a prevalent part of the discussion. Gorman states:

> "True community is more than being together. A person does not develop trust in others simply by being in a group where members study together, pray together, and share a common group leader. Trust involves relatedness. Relatedness is more than presence although that is the beginning. To relate, one

---

[98] Falwell and Dempsey. *Innovatechurch. Innovative leadership for the next generation church.* 114.

must know, and to know one must work at being open to trust."[99]

One will find that within community there are relationships built and grown in an intimate and loving manner. An example of this is found in the community of Jesus Christ and His disciples. Jesus utilized the small group format creating a community of disciples that lived together, and with the process of discipleship, they grew into an intimate and loving relationship with Jesus Christ and with each other.

Models of Discipleship - Biblical Foundations Relational Model

There are many different models of discipleship that have found their roots in the Bible. One of the first models that one can see clearly in the Bible is that found in the relationship between Jesus and His disciples. According to Coleman, "One cannot transform the world except as individuals in the world are transformed, and individuals cannot be changed except as they are molded in the hands of the Master."[100] Jesus walked, taught, and lived life with His disciples under the umbrella of a relationship. This relationship falls under the theme of community. This community that Jesus built with His disciples was

---

[99] Gorman, Julie. *Community That Is Christian: A Handbook On Small Groups.* Colorado Springs, CO: Chariot Victor. 1993. 43.
[100] Coleman, Robert E. *The Master Plan of Evangelism.* 2nd. ed. Grand Rapids, MI: Revel Publishing. 1993. 24.

constructed on the sharing of every aspect of life. Through this Relational Model approach, Jesus would change the world. Some may feel that this relationship may have ended upon the death of Jesus, but this model continued in their day as well into the present day. One can see this relationship with the resurrected Jesus through the disciples in the book of Acts. Luke brings this to life right from the beginning of this book. This relationship can be seen so clearly as the disciples were living a daily relationship with Jesus Christ as well as with each other.[101] This would be called a Relational Model of Discipleship. As stated by Zempel, "Within the Relational approach to discipleship, people grew in their relationship to Christ as they grew in their relationship to one another."[102] People growing in, and with, a community of people as they grow together in Christ Jesus, is the foundation of this approach. This model of discipleship seems to have lost its traction once there became a more institutional form of worship established under Constantine beginning around 312 A.D. However, this model has been extremely effective throughout history within the small group format of gatherings such as cell or community groups.

Academic Model

The second model of discipleship that needs a closer look is found in the area of academics. Many churches utilize

---

[101] Acts 2.
[102] Zempel, Heather. *Models of Discipleship Throughout Church History.* 2006. 1.

this form, or model, of discipleship through the formation of Sunday school and other programs that encourage the expanding of the mind through study. Zempel states, "In the academic approach to discipleship, people were taught about Christ and grew in their relationship to him through a systematic, academic approach."[103] Paul spoke of this model as he stated, "Do not conform any longer to the pattern of this world, but be transformed by the renewing of your mind."[104] One can see the word "transformed" as a result of the renewing of a person's mind. Any time one is involved in the study of the Word, this would qualify as discipleship. One can also see this as Luke states, "And they continued steadfastly in the apostles' doctrine and fellowship, and in breaking of bread, and in prayers."[105] Again, later in history, one finds the teachings of Pachomius. He is considered the father of community monasticism and required his monks to study. According to Smither, "Pachomius made scriptural teaching and memorization a vital part of the daily monastic program and encouraged his monks to read while following a Rule that had Scripture as its basis."[106] The academic model became very much a preferred manner with the invention of the printing press. As the Bible became more accessible

---

[103] Zempel, Heather. *Models of Discipleship Throughout History. 2006.* 2.

[104] Romans 12: 2.

[105] Acts 2: 42.

[106] Smither, Edward L. *Augustine as Mentor. A Model for Preparing Spiritual Leaders.* Nashville, TN: B&H Publishing Group. 2008. 51.

to the average man, he began to read it and join groups with teachers to gain knowledge.

Incarnational Model

The last model that needs to be examined would be called the Incarnational Model of Discipleship. This model can be found in the more theologically liberal churches of the 20th Centuries. According to Zempel, "These churches espoused a belief that Jesus' call to action on behalf of the poor, sick, and oppressed was the channel by which we learned about him, became more like him, and grew in our relationship with him."[107] Biblically, one sees the teachings of Jesus to care for those who are hungry, sick, or poor etc., but also, again, in the book of Acts one finds the disciples caring for others in this manner; "And sold their possessions and goods, and parted them to all men, as every man had need."[108] A central theme for those of this model demonstrate that caring for the less fortunate is how they grow in Christ and help others learn to grow in Jesus. Extending love to others is a wonderful way to show the love of Jesus and open the doors of a relationship to others. Once the lost person feels that a person really cares and loves them by their expressions of love, there can be a sharing of the gospel and an opportunity for others to find salvation in Christ. Fay states, "Nonbelievers must hear the gospel an average of 7.6 times before they receive

---

[107] Ibid. 2.
[108] Acts 2: 45.

it. So if anyone walks away from you when you share the gospel with him, remember: the Word of God never returns void...Your obedience to share may bring this person to a turning point."[109] So to have opportunities in the present day, many feel this is a model that will serve well for discipleship. Another area this model can be found is in the world missions. According to Moreau, "Incarnational Mission: Just as Christ was incarnated as a person, so missionaries, it can be said, need to incarnate themselves into a new context. They cannot come as newborns, but they can learn the language and culture of their new context in such a way that they can behave like one who was born in that context."[110]

The above three models of discipleship serve as Biblical foundations that one can build upon to reach and aid others in their Christian growth. Though there are many other models found in the Bible, these mentioned above can serve to help others understand that there are historical and Biblical basis for discipleship. As one studies these models, it is apparent that to be involved in a discipleship program, one must first be a disciple. This comes to each of us through the word that seems to come out abundantly clear in these models, and that is "transformation." One must be transformed by the blood of Jesus to be a disciple,

---

[109] Fay, William and Linda Evans Shepherd. *Share Jesus Without Fear*. Nashville, TN: B&H Publishing Group. 1999. 11.

[110] Moreau, A. Scott, Gary R. Corwin and Gary B. McGee. *Introducing World Missions: A Biblical, Historical and Practical Survey*. Grand Rapids, MI: Baker Academic Publishing. 2004. 12.

and then one's heart is transformed by the discipleship process as one grows into the likeness of Jesus.

Discipleship in the Gospels

To examine discipleship in the Gospels of the Bible, one would first need to examine the early leaders. The first Christian leader would be that of John the Baptist. Some might feel that we should begin with the person of Jesus but to illustrate how God wants to develop and send out His disciples, a close look at John will aid in this effort. As stated in His Word, "In those days came John the Baptist, preaching in the wilderness of Judea, And saying, Repent ye: for the kingdom of heaven is at hand."[111] His ministry was active and alive as he was preaching and baptizing for the repentance of sins. An interesting point on the above scripture is that the phrase "kingdom of heaven" is found only in the gospel of Matthew. The gospels of Mark and Luke use the phrase "kingdom of God" and most accept these terms to be used interchangeably but the phrase in Matthew was probably used this way as this gospel was written to the Jews and to say "God" may have been offensive so Matthew chose the word "heaven." The point was that John was speaking about the Messiah coming soon, so he was speaking as of a future event. This can be supported by the scripture "John answered, saying unto them all, I indeed baptize you with water; but

---

[111] Matthew 3: 1- 2.

one mightier than I cometh, the latchet of whose shoes I am not worthy to unloose: He shall baptize you with the Holy ghost and with fire."[112]

John the Baptist had disciples that followed him and participated in his ministry as supported by scripture, "Again the next day after John stood, and two of his disciples;"[113] However, once Jesus began His ministry, the disciples of John left him and joined the ministry of Jesus. Carson states, "but in the light of John the Baptist's self-perception as the forerunner of the Coming One, it is reasonable to assume that at least some of his disciples, those perhaps who understood him best, discerned that their master was constantly pointing beyond himself to another."[114] In effect, God separated and sent them out to continue to grow under the leadership of Jesus Christ. Then we see that they are again sent, after the crucifixion, as they are now prepared to go into the world and serve God.

Now our attention must be placed squarely on the person of Jesus Christ. Jesus was baptized by John the Baptist - suffered the temptation of Satan - and He began His ministry. The Scriptures support this as His Word says, "From that time Jesus began to preach, and to say, Repent: for the kingdom of heaven is at hand."[115] One

---

[112] Luke 3: 16.

[113] John 1: 35.

[114] Carson, D. A. *The Gospel According To John: The Pillar New Testament Commentary.* Grand Rapids, MI: Wm. B. Eerdmans Publishing Company. 1991. 154.

[115] Matthew 4: 17.

can find a more descriptive statement of Jesus from His Word as it states, "And saying, the time is fulfilled, and the kingdom of God is at hand: repent ye, and believe the gospel."[116] Unlike John who spoke of a future event, Jesus states His kingdom is now. Jesus then begins to call his twelve disciples together for discipleship and training.

This must be understood that the disciples answered the call of God to repent and be saved. Once they were called, left their lives, families, and work, they entered a community of God and into a community with each other. Though Jesus preached to many, His discipleship training was done in a small community of believers. From this understanding, one can see the Relational Model of Discipleship used by Jesus Christ for His disciples. For three and half years, the disciples walked, ate, talked, trained, and lived with the person of Jesus Christ. One can see the training and discipleship of Jesus to His disciples in many ways. Jesus encouraged Nathanael from the beginning, He loved John as He allowed him to lie on His chest, He tolerated the doubts of Thomas, and He rebuked Peter. Ultimately, Jesus was building eleven men to be ready to be sent out into the world. As He changed them, they would go out, with the power of the Holy Spirit, and change the world.

Jesus gave them and all Christians much needed information. Jesus was clear that His disciples needed to understand that God loved them and that they

---

[116] Mark 1: 5.

needed to love Him first! Jesus gives them the "Great Commandment;" - "Jesus said unto him, Thou shalt love the Lord thy God with all thy heart, and with all thy soul, and with all thy mind. This is the first and great commandment."[117] It was clear that there needed to be love of God first and foremost! Love is essential to the life of a Christian. Jesus then gave His disciples another understanding of His teachings. This is found as Jesus gives them the "New Commandment;" "A new commandment I give unto you, that ye love one another; as I have loved you, that ye also love one another."[118] According to Dempsey, "Here Jesus takes love one step further. We are to love God. We are to love our neighbor. And in God's plan we are to love other brothers and sisters in Christ. Love is the central component in the kingdom of God. God loves us and sent His son. As a result we can love God."[119] The last recorded passage of Jesus to His disciples can be found in the "Great Commission;" "Go ye therefore, and teach all nations, baptizing them in the name of the Father, and of the Son, and of the Holy Ghost: Teaching them to observe all things whatsoever I have commanded you: and, lo, I am with you alway, even unto the end of the world. Amen."[120] This is an amazing statement to His disciples, and to all disciples. Jesus sends His disciples out on His mission!

---

[117] Matthew 22: 37 – 38.

[118] John 13: 34 – 35.

[119] Falwell, Jonathan. Gen. Ed. Dempsey, Rod. *Innovatechurch. 2008.* 105.

[120] Matthew 28: 19 – 20.

Mission is a vital part of the discipleship process. One finds that God Himself is the author of missions. Jesus Incarnate was the first true missionary as He left heaven in submission to the Father, as He was "sent" to bring salvation to man. In the words of Jesus Christ Himself, one finds this truth as He states, "For I came down from heaven, not to do mine own will, but the will of him that sent me."[121] Though God called and sent men like Abraham and Moses, one sees that Jesus is the first true missionary as He was sent by the Father from heaven and He accomplished His mission in the physical. Jesus is sent by the Father and gathers and builds disciples to be sent out on their mission. On His mission, He brought together other disciples (apostles) and brought them into a small community and developed them for their mission. An interesting point is found in the word "apostle." According to Elwell, "The biblical use of "apostle" is almost entirely confined to the NT, where it occurs seventy-nine times: ten in the Gospels, twenty-eight in Acts, thirty-eight in the epistles, and three in the Apocalypse. Our English word is a transliteration of the Greek *apostolos,* derived from *apostellein* (to send)."[122] In His Word Jesus states, "Then said Jesus to them again, Peace be unto you: as my Father hath sent me, even so send I you."[123] Another interesting point for this

---

[121] John 6: 38.

[122] Elwell, Walter A. *Evangelical Dictionary of Theology,* 2nd ed. Grand Rapids, MI: Baker Academic. 2001. 85.

[123] John 20: 21.

discussion is found in the understanding of "*Missio Dei* which is Latin for "the sending of God"...In sum, *Missio Dei* is a comprehensive term encompassing everything God does in relation to the kingdom and everything the church is sent to do on earth."[124] It is clear in the Gospels that Jesus was sent by His Father on mission and Jesus sent His apostles on mission to the glory of God.

Discipleship in the book of Acts

The book of Acts is overflowing with historical evidence of Christian discipleship. One of the first passages that aid in the revelation of discipleship is found at the hand of God. Jesus has instructed His disciples to wait for the "promise of the Father." God sends His Holy Spirit to the men and women in the upper room empowering them to begin their mission for Christ. The resurrected Jesus Christ speaks to these disciples, "But ye shall receive power, after that the Holy Ghost is come upon you: and ye shall be witnesses unto me both in Jerusalem, and in all Judea, and in Samaria, and unto the uttermost part of the earth."[125] One can clearly see that these disciples of Jesus Christ are to wait for the promise of God in the Holy Spirit to be "sent" to them. However, once they receive this promise, they would become witnesses for Jesus Christ all over the earth. This is considered the map

---

[124] Moreau, Corwin, and McGee. *Introducing World Missions: A Biblical, Historical, and Practical Survey.* 73.
[125] Acts 1: 8.

(geography) for all disciples on where they are to go out and it is one of the five Great Commissions found in the Bible.

One can clearly see the revelation of this promise as the disciples were gathered together in the upper room awaiting the promise of the Father. As found in His Word, "And suddenly there came a sound from heaven as of a rushing mighty wind, and it filled all the house where they were sitting."[126] The disciples receive the outpouring of the promise of God and began their mission and their ministry. As they begin this mission, there is strong evidence of all of the disciples being of one accord and continued in the teaching of the Word of God, fellowshipping together, sharing meals together, and in prayers together. These people were following the same format that Jesus Christ led His disciples in their discipleship. They were learning, sharing life in fellowship and meals, and praying together; "And they continued steadfastly in the apostles' doctrine and fellowship, and in breaking of bread, and in prayers."[127] Again, one can see the theme of community within the Scriptures as the disciples lived life together and shared this life in every way. According to Scriptures, it is clear that the discipleship by God through the apostles to others was administered in both the temple and in the small family/community gatherings as seen in the words of Luke, "And

---

[126] Acts 2: 2.
[127] Acts 2: 42.

they, continuing daily with one accord in the temple, and breaking bread from house to house, did eat their meat with gladness and singleness of heart."[128] Again, as seen in the discipleship of Jesus in the Gospels toward His apostles, now His apostles are forming small groups to administer the discipleship to others in small groups also.

Though this is an important point in the understanding of the history of Christian discipleship, its revelation of the effectiveness may be needed. They would go to the temple for the preaching, teaching, and exhorting others which is an important facet of the discipleship process. However, one may need to reflect on the definition of discipleship to refresh the memories to understand the other part the apostles were accomplishing at this time. Early/Dempsey state their definition of discipleship is, ""Discipleship is the process of guiding individual disciples to grow in spiritual maturity and to discover and use their gifts, talents and abilities in fulfillment of Christ's mission."[129]

Discipleship is a process, so the need for temple was important, but so was the small house group. Arnold says, "Whether house churches were independent groups of believers or were part of larger churches is uncertain. It is likely, however, that small house fellowships were the building blocks of the church in each city or region."[130] In today's environment in America, the local New Testament

---

[128] Acts 2: 46.

[129] Falwell, Jonathan. Gen. Ed. Dempsey, Rod. *Innovate church.* 2008. 112.

[130] Arnold, Jeffrey. *The Big Book on Small Groups.* Downers Grove, IL: InterVarsity Press. 1992. 18.

church is important and should consist of small groups. There needed to be a certain element of intimacy between the members of the group to accomplish this task. The process of guiding individuals in spiritual growth in the praying together and confessing of sins together requires this intimacy. Also, the discovery and development of spiritual gifts, talents and abilities can be heightened under the more close and personal attention of others.

It is also very clear that this model of Christian discipleship pleased God. Twice in Acts 2, one can see God blessing the public preaching of Peter as God adds about three thousand souls to His church. Also, God adds daily to His church following the small house gathering descriptions from Scripture, "Praising God, and having favor with all the people. And the Lord added to the church daily such as should be saved."[131]

However, with the onset of this exciting time came much persecution of Christians. The book of Acts illustrates the persecution of Christians from the imprisonment of Peter and John, the killing and stoning of Stephen, and the Jews seeking to kill Saul to name but just a few. According to Stark, "During the summer of the year 64, the emperor Nero sometimes lit up his garden at night by setting fire to a few fully conscious Christians who had been covered with wax and then impaled high on poles forced up their rectums. Nero also had Christians killed by wild animals in the arena, and he even crucified a

---

[131] Acts 2: 47.

few."[132] As the persecutions continued, the house churches/ gatherings also continued. According to Mallison, "It is almost certain that every mention of a local church or meeting, whether for worship or fellowship, is in actual fact a reference to a church meeting in a house."[133] The small group/church gatherings were being persecuted but they were not dying out. They simply continued serving God by serving others by the continuing of the discipleship process. It appears that as those who hated the Christians of this time and wanted to destroy them all, this persecution may have made them stronger by forcing them to band together in strength. According to Buchanan, "The persecution eventually escalated to the place where the believers were driven underground. They were greatly dependent on each other and perhaps lived in closer relationships with each other than at any previous time."[134]

Discipleship in the Epistles

It is clear how the theme of community reigns through the book of Acts and one can see that this theme continues in the writings of Paul in the Epistles. Paul burst on the scene in the book of Acts and became one of the greatest missionaries in the history of Christianity. He

---

[132] Stark, Rodney. *the Triumph of Christianity.* 2011. 137.

[133] Comiskey, Joel. *The Joel Comiskey Group.* *http://www.joelcomiskeygroup.com/articles/dissertation/History.html. 2015.*

[134] Buchanan, Rodney. *History of Pre-Reformation Small Groups.* Article used by Dr. Dempsey at Liberty University Class. 2015.

was one of the greatest church planters also. He either began most churches with his presence, or under his influence or teachings of disciples, that went out to begin their churches. According to Cole, "To the Colossians, he writes a letter as the apostle of this expanding Asian network, but he also mentions that they, along with the Laodicean church, have never seen his face."[135]

The apostles obeyed Jesus Christ as He told them to wait on God to receive His power to go out and witness so others could believe in Jesus Christ as the Messiah. Churches were springing up all over the known world as the apostles engaged their disciples in the process of discipleship. However, one of the greatest, Paul, was apparently under the same discipleship process of Jesus Christ that the apostles underwent, and it changed his life and the life of Christianity. Scriptures records it this way, "For I neither received it of man, neither was I taught it, but by the revelation of Jesus Christ."[136]

Persecution continued to reign against the early Christians, however, they continued to flourish and grow. Throughout the Epistles one can see that the house church continued in many cities, such as, Jerusalem, Rome, Corinth, Ephesus, and Galatia to name but a few. Sometimes, there may be only one house church; however, as Paul greets them in his letters, one sees that he

---

[135] Cole, Neil. *Church 3.0: upgrades for the future of the church.* San Francisco, CA: Jossey-Bass. 2010. 111.
[136] Galatians 1: 12.

uses the plural of church. There were a number of house churches in a city such as in his letter to Galatia; "And all the brethren which are with me, unto the churches of Galatia."[137] To the many churches recognized in the Bible, one can see that Paul was a great church planter. However, he was a strong believer in the discipleship process set forth by Jesus Christ. One simply needs to look at the example of Jesus Christ to find the template of discipleship. Paul believed strongly that his disciples can look through him to Jesus Christ as their leader. Scriptures give strong support to this as it states, "Timothy who is my beloved son, and faithful in the Lord, who shall bring you into remembrance of my ways which be in Christ, as I teach everywhere in every church."[138] This was a foundation on which he utilized in his discipleship process. One can find this in another Scripture; "Be ye followers of me, even as I also am of Christ."[139] There is sound advice found from the author of the book of Hebrews as he states, "Jesus Christ the same yesterday, and today, and forever."[140] According to Willard, "...that the nature of discipleship to Jesus and its outcomes does not change."[141]

Again, one finds the theme of community being used

---

[137] Galatians 1: 2.

[138] 1 Corinthians 4; 17.

[139] 1 Corinthians 11: 1.

[140] Hebrews 13: 8.

[141] Willard, Dallas. *Discipleship. http://www.dwillard.org/articles/artview. asp?artID=134.* Article for the Oxford Handbook of Evangelical Theology, edited by Gerald McDermott, 2010. 5.

in the Epistles is from the foundation and example of that community of Jesus Christ. A close look at what is called "The Great Plan," and "The Great Ambition," found in the book of Ephesians and in the book of Colossians is how God, through Paul, communicated the use of the roles of both leaders and the body. This is such an important area to understand in the discipleship process as in the Great Plan, one finds that God calls His pastors to equip the saints for service and how He fits the body together with His children for growth.[142] This discipleship process for the body involves the discovery and development of their spiritual gifts. According to Dempsey, "This involves the disciple discovering and developing his or her gift and developing in the body (community) to their full potential."[143] Also, in the Great Ambition, one finds that it is the ambition of the leaders to develop each and every disciple so that they be presented complete to Jesus.[144] If one follows the prescription of Paul on these areas, it is clear that discipleship must be directed to each individual person in the body of Christ to grow them to be complete and if this can be accomplished, the church as a whole will grow.

---

[142] Ephesians 4: 11 – 16.
[143] Dempsey, Rod. *Innovatechurch. 2008. 108.*
[144] Colossians 1: 28.

Discipleship down through the centuries

As one looks at the history of Christian discipleship throughout the centuries, it would be advisable to begin with the ministry of Jesus Christ! As it has been examined in the above work, Jesus Christ is the example that everything must be compared with, and to. The theme of community that Jesus set forth in the first century is one that has continued throughout the centuries.

As the community is the template for a strong discipleship, it has grown even stronger during periods of persecution. An important point on the understanding of community is according to Anderson, "A community revolves around something shared: a neighborhood, business, political cause, medical issue, sport, hobby."[145] As Anderson stated, communities over the centuries shared a common interest in the area of political cause which was expressed in the manner of persecution. This would seem to draw them closer to God and closer to each other. One can see this clearly in the present day in the countries of China, North Korea, and Sudan to name but a few. However, the small communities are continuing to grow in strength and in numbers in the country of China which can be attributed to the power of God and His power found in each community. Again, Anderson states, "There were more martyrs for Jesus

---

[145] Anderson, Leith. *The Jesus Revolution: Learning from Christ's First Followers.* Nashville, TN: Abingdon Press. 2009. 20.

Christ in the twentieth century than in all the previous nineteen centuries combined. In the twenty-first century, there is persecution in Vietnam, North Korea, China, Sudan, and many other countries."[146] So this has been with Christians for centuries but somehow God seems to turn persecution to His glory.

Another area that had an impact on the Christian and discipleship can be found in the year of 313, and the Roman Emperor Constantine. Though Constantine had many wonderful influences on and for Christians, he also had some negative effects. One of the positive affects Constantine had was that he elevated Christianity to a State Religion and this help reduce the persecution against the Christians. Though many of this time thought this was a good thing, history shows that it also had negative effects. One of the negative effects can be found in how Constantine made some major changes within Christianity. According to Stark, "But Constantine's major contribution was to elevate the clergy to high levels of wealth, power, and status."[147] This feudalistic influence has lasted until the present day. Constantine also aided in the commissioning of the construction of many buildings of which one is the St. Peter's Basilica, along with many others. One of the major negative effects on Christian discipleship is that people began to leave the examples of Jesus in community and came to focus on the buildings

---

[146] Ibid. 59.
[147] Stark, Rodney. *the Triumph of Christianity.* 2011. 174.

and hierarchical structure of the church instead of the intimate and loving need to grow in Christ.

This continued until the time of Reformation ushered in by Martin Luther. Though the Reformation had a huge impact in many different areas of Christianity, this author only wants to focus on that of discipleship. Again, in reflection to the above mentioned making of disciples, true Reformation began when Martin Luther became reborn into the family of God. God was working and in the process of discipleship with Martin Luther as he stumbled over the Scripture; "For I am not ashamed of the gospel of Christ: for it is the power of God unto salvation to everyone that believeth; to the Jew first, and also to the Greek. For therein is the righteousness of God revealed from faith to faith as it is written, the just shall live by faith."[148] Martin Luther soon realized that the church couldn't save a person; it was only by faith in Jesus Christ. According to Stark, "Most radical of all, Luther proposed that salvation is God's gift, freely given, and is gained entirely by faith in Jesus as the redeemer."[149] It is amazing that Stark chose the words "...gained entirely by faith in Jesus..." as this is precisely what Luther stumbled onto. According to Dillenberger, "human activity no longer has any part in the ultimate determination of man's destiny. Grace alone enables man to stand before the righteousness

---

[148] Romans 1: 16 – 17.
[149] Ibid. 319.

of God."[150] In a nutshell approach that is narrowed toward discipleship, Martin Luther stood against the church that wasn't concerned with the discipleship and growth of their congregations into the likeness of Jesus Christ but more focused on their money and power. In his way, Martin Luther was victorious in his stand to show the people that they must become disciples of Jesus Christ if they want to grow in His discipleship. Luther stood on both sides of the issue of small groups. He first came out in favor of small groups and the need for intimacy and growth found in small groups. This can be found in his sound teaching on the area of the priesthood of believers. However, later in his life he reversed his position.

Any examination of the subject of history of Christian discipleship wouldn't be complete without a short discussion of two men. The first is Philip Jacob Spener who is known as the father of Pietism. The small group environment for discipleship was essential to Pietism. According to Buchanan, "His most important contribution was a reform of the practical life of the churches, which included the concept of small groups designed for spiritual growth."[151] Spener was a champion of having a covenant relationship within the small group for accountability to God and each other!

The second man that needs to be mentioned is that of

---

[150] Dillenberger, John. *Martin Luther: Selections from His Writings.* New York, NY: Anchor Books. 1962. xviii.

[151] Buchanan, Rodney. *History of Pre-Reformation Small Groups.* 2015.

John Wesley. Though Wesley was heavily influenced by the Puritans and Pietists, he was a giant of a man for God. He too followed in the footsteps of small groups that were laid out before him. However, he took this to another level in the development of what Wesley called, society, class, and bands. The larger groups being society and they separated into the class groups, and then a smaller group called bands came out of class groups. Each of these groups had a distinct usefulness and meaning. Along with Spener, Wesley held that the covenant relationship was tremendously important, on the corporate level but also to the individual.

Today, in American churches, the people are free to worship where and whom they choose as there was a rejection of a State Church Religion. Many American Churches today strive to reach and teach their people, to the glory of God. However, there is a noticeable breakdown in this line of communication. It is a known fact that over 80% of American Churches are failing as they are either in a state of plateau or in decline. One of the factors of decline is that the feudalistic foundation continues to remain in our American Churches of today. The leaders today continue to keep the people focused on themselves, their buildings and their religion. This continues to help keep the eyes of the people off the person of Jesus Christ. If the eyes of the people are not on the person of Jesus Christ, one can bet that the hearts are far away from Him also. As one looks at the history of Christian discipleship, it is apparent that this theme of community is strong, yet very few churches utilize this method of discipleship.

History of Small Groups

A brief look at the history of small groups, or sometimes called cell groups, will provide valuable information to the understanding of how this vehicle can be the driving force of discipleship. Beckham makes a powerful statement concerning small groups as he says, "The strongest organizational unit in the world's history would appear to be that which we call a cell because it is a remorseless self-multiplier; is exceptionally difficult to destroy; can preserve its intensity of local life while vast organizations quickly wither when they are weakened at the center; can defy the power of governments; is the appropriate lever of prising open any status quo."[152] One can see the power in the small group from the discussion of Jethro to Moses in the Old Testament[153] as well in the New Testament, especially in Acts.[154] The small group is recorded many times as this served as the New Testament house church. Mallison states, "It is almost certain that every mention of a local church or meeting, whether for worship or fellowship, is in actual fact a reference to a

---

[152] Beckham, William A. *The Two-Winged Church Will Fly.* Houston, TX: Touch Publications. 1993. 119.

[153] Exodus 18: 14 – 23.

[154] Acts 2: 42 – 47.

church meeting in a house."[155] This can be seen in the book of Acts 12: 12, as Mary, the mother of Mark, opens her house in Jerusalem as well as the service of Priscilla and Aquila as mentioned in the epistles. Viola states, "One of the most striking marks of the early church was the absence of special religious buildings...In fact, the early church was the only religious group in the first century that met exclusively in the homes of its members."[156] The early Christians lived in community as were the examples of the apostles in the book of Acts. Hood states, "The early church lived in community and shared everything they had. Read the book of Acts. There was nothing easy or comfortable about the church being the church in a Christless culture."[157] Living in community utilizing the small group format was not easy and it was an effective method of building disciples.

A major change that occurred in history that did have an effect upon the small groups that met as house churches found in the Bible is seen in the life of the Roman Emperor, Constantine. In the year 312 A.D., the Roman Emperor Constantine, being converted to the Christian faith, decided to make Christianity the State Religion. According to Ferguson, "Since there was one supreme

---

[155] Mallison, John. *Growing Christians in Small Groups. Homebush West, N.S.W: ANZEA Publishers. 1989.* 5.

[156] Viola, Frank. *Reimagining Church: Pursuing the Dream of Organic Christianity.* Colorado Springs, CO: David C. Cook Publishing. 2008. 86 – 87.

[157] Hood, Pat. *The Sending Church: The Church Must Leave the Building.* Nashville, TN: B&H Publishing Group. 2013. 18.

God, Constantine felt there should be one earthly rule corresponding to the one divine rule. His mission was to overcome the demons of barbarians without the divisions within associated with polytheism."[158] This ended many years of Christian persecution by the Roman government. One of the major public emphases was found in the building of many chapels/basilicas that gave Christians the opportunity to worship in public and not only in their houses. Ferguson states, "Perhaps the greatest outward show of favor for the church was Constantine's extensive building program."[159] In the building of the many structures for the Christians, it did reduce the small groups and replace the community church. This can be seen in history as well as into the present modern-day worship of Christians.

There does seem to be a few voices in the wilderness that are calling out for the return to the first century small group format. Cole says, "Every Christian is a church planter, every home is a church, and every church building is a training center."[160] It is apparent that Cole's vision is that of returning to the small group format that was so effective in the process of discipleship in the early church. So, if every Christian is a church planter, then it goes without saying that the Christian that plants the church would be the leader of that church. Jesus said in

---

[158] Ferguson, Everett. *Church History, Volume One: From Christ to Pre-Reformation.* Grand Rapids, MI: Zondervan. 2005. 186.

[159] Ibid. 184.

[160] Cole, Neil. *Organic Church.* 2005. xxvi – xxvii.

Matthew 16:18, "...Thou art Peter, and upon this rock I will build my church; and the gates of hell shall not prevail against it."[161] The actual word used in this Scripture for the English word "church" is the Greek word *ekklesia*. This Greek word when one boils it down simply means the people of God. So, Jesus is saying He will build His people of God and the gates of hell shall not prevail. Jesus is always building His people to transform them into His likeness. Rainer and Geiger say, "As a church leader, you partner with God to build the lives of people. If God has given you a clear process for making and maturing disciples, you must focus on the one thing in your church."[162] Small groups are an effective way to build disciples.

One of the main reasons for the effectiveness of small groups can be found in the intimacy of community. A close-knit group of people living, learning, and growing together in Christ. According to Donahue and Robinson, "This is what God dreams for us and our churches. We are called to move into community, one at a time, on the basis of God's identity as Three in One...We must find ways to answer that call by creating an expanding network of small groups. That is the theological case. The evidence is overwhelming."[163] It is clear that the small

---

[161] Matthew 16:18

[162] Rainer, Thom S. and Eric Geiger. *Simple Church: Returning To God's Process For Making Disciples.* Nashville, TN: B&H Publishing Group. 2011. 202.

[163] Donahue, Bill and Russ Robinson. *Building A Church of Small Groups: a place where nobody stands alone.* Grand Rapids, MI: Zondervan. 2001. 32.

group must identify with the Triune God and living and growing in community is an important element in the discipleship process. Growing in Christ is important and to accomplish this, a small group must facilitate the growth in the knowledge of God's Word. A disciple must be grounded in the word of God to walk the walk of a disciple and not faint. Arnold states:

"Within a relationship-building framework, a primary task of the community of Christ is to know what God wants. So, we must learn to read and apply God's Word with integrity. Small group study is a human community's effort to glean God-to-human truth through the help of the Holy Spirit."[164]

Another area of importance is found in the area of evangelizing. All disciples are commanded to go into the world and make disciples. The going process is the mission and making disciples cannot happen without evangelization. Evangelization is the proclaiming of the good news of Jesus Christ to the world. According to Arnold, "God also works in and through the life of a witness…Our response to God's role in the process of evangelism is simple – obedience…God uses witnesses who are willing to reach out in humility, love and confidence."[165] A disciple must be trained to obey God and go out and make disciples. What better place to

---

[164] Arnold, Jeffrey. *The Big Book on Small Groups.* Downers Grove, IL: InterVarsity Press. 1992. 43.
[165] Ibid. 168.

bring a person who has just received the good news of Jesus Christ and has been reborn but to a small group that teaches discipleship? In community, a person finds the intimacy to be open and honest and grows with each other. A new Christian would have many questions and may feel strange to be discussing them with strangers but once introduced to a small group, it would be a short time before the person finds the intimacy and security to be open. Johnson states, "One way to build a sense of togetherness and closeness is by being sensitive to members' needs and joining together to meet these needs...Sharing what we are thinking and feeling can bind us together with a sense of having common experiences and feelings."[166] As disciples, what could be more common than the salvation experience and sharing of this experience only brings about intimacy and closeness that aids in the growth of disciples.

There is one word that I would like to add to the small group format and that is the word *missional!* Jesus was on a mission when He came out of heaven and that mission was given to Him by His Father. Jesus then commands the disciples to "Go" into the world and make disciples and they, too, were on mission. We all are to be involved in the making of disciples through the small *missional* group format. God will dictate your group's vision and it will be different for each group but ultimately, your

---

[166] Johnson, Judy. *Good Things Come in Small Groups: The Dynamics of Good Group Life.* Downers Grove, IL: InterVarsity Press. 1985. 102 – 103.

mission will glorify God through the making of disciples. This is a vital part of all small groups and without the mission, you will only be a small group of people. When you allow God to add the mission to your group, you become a dangerous small group of people with a mission from God to reach the world!

These are simply some of the reasons that small group missional format is effective and how the small group format facilitates the process of discipleship. A close-knit group of people with common interests to grow in Christ and on mission to make disciples is a powerful group. It does not surprise me that these are some of the same reasons that Jesus Christ chose this format to the development of His disciples. Clearly, the apostles followed in His footsteps and utilized the same small group format for the discipleship process that led to them sending disciples out into the world. The small group missional format was, and is, an effective vehicle for making disciples and the church needs to embrace this method once again.

Chapter 6

"Let Reformation Begin"

"All scripture is given by inspiration of God and is profitable for doctrine, for reproof, for correction, for instruction in righteousness: That the man of God may be perfect, thoroughly furnished unto all good works."
2 Timothy 3: 16

Clearly, armed with all the supporting information from the previous chapters, you will agree that most Churches in America are either dying or dead. However, after speaking to many people on this subject, many still love to resist and push back saying, "maybe this is true but that's not the case in my church!" You may find yourself fighting back against the truth and saying this exact statement to me at this time. Knowing that many can feel this way and knowing that anyone that feels this way won't be open to the truth, I felt it imperative to give you a test. Let's check and see exactly how healthy your church is today.

I will examine seven areas of the church and explain

how the Bible tells us how we are to do things and then, we will ask you for your honest opinion by checking a 'YES' or 'NO' at the end of each section. We will calculate your score and if your church is either dying or a dead church, you will then know the truth. I only ask that if you find that your church is dying or dead that you will immediately call a meeting of your church and either develop a small group discussion on this book and discuss the results to become reformed or that you take steps to revival, which ever you feel is appropriate after seeking God for His guidance. Deal? Great!

I hope at this point in the book that you will agree with me that the American Church is in a death spiral and this is due to man's sin of disobedience. Most of us understand that when we are in sin, we must confess, repent, and be forgiven for our sins by, and in, the blood of Jesus Christ. Sin separates man from God and this is now very clear that this has occurred on a corporate level in the church.

The American Church needs reformation and it must come from the acceptance of the Word of God. Martin Luther was faced in a life or death struggle with the Catholic Church. His desire was not to reject the Catholic Church, but his desire was that the Catholic Church would be reformed by the Word of God and they would begin to operate in the Will of God found in the Word of God. Many credit Martin Luther with reformation but Luther states, "I did nothing; the Word did everything." [167]

It is my sincere desire that before we proceed into the remaining chapters of this book, which can bring hope, reformation and revival to God's church, we must stop and confess our sins to God and each other. We must repent and turn from our sins and turn to God and be forgiven of our sins. If we do this, I believe God will send forth the Holy Spirit with the power of reconciliation and bring forth His Church to bless man! We will examine this in more detail, and I hope this will be a blessing to you and your church.

I must tell you that I had no idea where the data that I collected would take me as I conducted my research for my Thesis Project for my Doctor of Ministry Degree (also called a dissertation in a Ph.D. program). In my research, I interviewed twenty local pastors/leaders of churches in Northern Arkansas and the results broke my heart. I asked each pastor/leader if they were saved and they all stated "yes." I asked each pastor/leader if they were called into this ministry position and all, but one said, "yes." The one said he wasn't called by God but was just trying to help his church. I asked each pastor/ leader if they were in the process of making disciples and though many had different understandings of the term "disciples," and after we agreed on a specific definition,

---

[167] Joel R. Beeke, *Scripture & the Legacy of the Reformation.* Gospel Reformation Network. 2017. Gospelreformation.net accessed on March 24, 2019.

every pastor/leader stated they were not making disciples in their church under their leadership! I offered each of them the opportunity to confess this as sin, repent from this sin, and to be forgiven, and to a man, not one pastor/leader accepted my offer. I even asked them to clarify this issue, if a congregant came to them and confessed they were in an adulterous affair, would they offer them the path to freedom of sin through confession, repentance, and forgiveness, and every pastor/leader stated "yes." I again offered them an opportunity to confess the sin of not making disciples and to repent and be forgiven, and every pastor/leader *REJECTED* that offer. Amazing but true! I hope this, though a small sample size of research data, does give a glimpse into the truth about the dying of the American Church!

I, also, must tell you that in my attempts to serve God by serving the church over the last five years, I have been rejected for many different reasons including fear.

> "If the world hates you, ye know that it hated me before it hated you. If ye were of the world, the world would love his own: but because ye are not of the world, but I have chosen you out of the world, therefore the world hateth you. Remember the word that I said unto you, the servant is not greater than his lord. If they have persecuted me, they will also persecute you, if they have kept

my saying, they will keep yours also." John
15: 18-20

I have been labeled, judged, and rejected by pastors
and leadership of the church as they have fought hard
against the truth. Allow me to remind you that I was
raised in my teenage years in the Detroit, Michigan area.
Have you ever been to the Detroit, Michigan area? That
is one tough place to live. The people are cold, distant and
fearful of others. I'm not saying there aren't some good
people, and maybe some good Christian people that live
in that area, but I am saying that the culture of Detroit
is a cold and distant culture. It is very hard to connect
with others in this area. Imagine how hard it would be
to connect with another and connect them to the person
of Jesus Christ? You do expect people from the Detroit
area to be cold, distant, and hard to relate too. I am from
this area of the country and yet, the scariest place on
earth that I have lived is in the Bible Belt of Arkansas.
That may surprise you, but I was so excited to move to
this area of Arkansas because I expected the culture to be
one of warmth, loving, closeness, and Christian! I was so
wrong. Most of the people of this culture are very hard to
connect with as they have a fear that if you are not part
of their family, you could cause harm to them. They push
you away and exclude you from their lives and families.
Many are the nicest people to your face and say things
like "Bless your heart" or "Sweet as Pie," but when you

turn you back, they are cold and cunning to keep you in your place.

Oh, by the way, if you are a Yankee, forget about it! Vicki and I attended a Methodist Church in rural Arkansas, and we met a man in Sunday School, and he asked where we lived. I told him we live in Mt. Pleasant, Arkansas and I had moved from Detroit, Michigan a few years earlier. He wasted no time and said, "Yankees are like hemorrhoids, if they come down and go back up, we think they are ok, but if they come down and stay, well, we don't like them at all." This absolute stranger tells me this story in two minutes after I meet him in a *CHURCH!* At this point you may be thinking I'm making this up but as God is my witness, he said that. Can you believe the love?

I always thought this culture was so loving and good and I was excited to join other Christians in their churches, but to be honest – they, for the most part, don't want anyone in their church that they don't know as family or a verified friend of the family.

Vicki and I attended another Baptist Church in Arkansas and they probably have about 200 people attend their church on a Sunday morning. We only attended this church for about two weeks when we noticed on this one Sunday morning, out of the approximate 200 people that attended church, *NOT ONE PERSON SAID GOOD MORNING OR EVEN SPOKE TO US.* I'm not making this stuff up. I'm a very outgoing person and have never met a stranger and I guess you could say I have the gift of gab. Well, this church absolutely didn't want us to attend with them, they wouldn't even say hello.

I had met the pastor of this church and told him how passionate I was about the need to make disciples and I wanted to connect with him to see if he felt the same and if there was a possibility of us working together on this issue that haunts most churches. He was so nice on the phone and then I met him on a Sunday night service, and he was so warm and friendly but guess what – you guessed it – He lied to me. He had told me he was interested in exploring this issue on the phone and he would call me the next week to set up a time to meet and I never heard from him again! A pastor who is caught in a lie. How could this be? Well, I hope you understand by now, if the heart of church lies and the people of the church are so dead and cold, you can understand why we grieve God so much.

Sadly, I have met with many pastors in Arkansas and had to begin my conversation with "I want to begin by telling you that I am not called as a pastor and *I DO NOT WANT YOUR JOB.*" However, the more pastors I met the more convinced that I became that the fear of the truth drove them away from me. They considered me a threat to their power or their money. Hmmm – who else does that sound like that had that same experience? Jesus walked on this earth only to bring love to a broken world and He offered it in a way that leaders couldn't understand so they did what they do when they can't control something or someone – *THEY KILLED HIM*!

Allow me to share another story about a meeting I had with a church leader from yet another Baptist Church in Arkansas. Vicki and I attended and even joined this church and spent approximately six months in church attendance. First, we both noticed that every week that only the greeters of this church would spend any time in conversation and mostly it was because I would engage them and not that they engaged us. The people of this church would simply go to service and then leave quickly and quietly. Cold and Distant! I had noticed that the music service was a powerful and inspiring time of worship, but the pastor refused to ever offer the gospel of Jesus Christ in his sermon messages. This was a growing church, approximately 400-500 people attended it, and I would say it qualified as a "feel good" church. You won't hear the gospel, but the message was offered like the message from Joel Osteen, a feel-good message but it never brought glory to God or true blessings to the people in need.

After meeting with the leader of this church a number of times and discussing the poor health of his church and the lack of discipleship, in which he agreed were major issues that they were going to address sometime, I asked him if he was interested in getting right with God and addressing the problems now – he said *NO*! I asked why not, and I will say that this man was very honest and open, he said, we have this huge new building and if I introduce something that makes people nervous they might leave the church and I can't pay my church building off. I asked him if this simply was a question of money and he said YES. I must admit, I really like this person as a man, but to deny God by rejecting His word and truth and doing church man's way will not profit a man but only bring disaster.

I admit that I have felt this way many times as I have attempted to share the truth. It isn't a comfortable feeling when you know you are a true threat to a man's power, position, and/or money. I say this to tell you that when I talked with pastors/leaders of churches, I didn't realize that I was putting them in a defensive posture. I thought by informing them of the fact that I wasn't a threat, they would lower their defenses and we could have a healthy exchange of some ideas that could bring glory to God and blessings to the church.

What I found was a much higher defensive position than I had expected. If I was right, the church would question why their pastor hadn't fixed the problem before now and fire him, or, if I was successful, they would give me credit and he would lose power and/or his job. That was never my intention! My only intention was to help the church find a new way to do God's Church by the Biblical examples left for us by the 1st Century leaders. That concept never made it off the launching pad!

I must tell you that when you are considered a threat

to the establishment, I always find comfort in knowing I was in the best company, Jesus and Martin Luther, as well as many other men and women over the years. It is time to come to the truth before it is too late!

In the following six chapters, we will explore six major issues that must be addressed by reformation to bring glory to God. The church problems are just small and simple in nature that a meeting of the church could bring change. These are huge issues that require everyone in the church to step up as the Body of Christ and, in humbleness, confess sin to God and each other. Repent of the sin by turning *away from* sin and *to* God for forgiveness, and begin to allow God the Holy Spirit to operate and lead His church and man needs to learn to follow Him.

The time for reformation has come! I must be brutally honest – It is time to begin to do God's Church – God's Way. Far too long man has operated God's Church – his way.

Chapter 7

Making Disciples in Today's Culture

"…one of His disciples said unto Him, Lord, teach
us to pray, as John also taught his disciples."
Luke 11: 1

Church Problem # 1:

The greatest problem that faces the Church of America
today is the issue of sin. The sin of disobedience is
killing the church. As discussed previously, the sin of
disobedience in the church by refusing to make disciples
and leaders of disciples as commanded by Jesus Christ is
a major problem. We have revealed the truth to you in its
entirety, so I will not spend any more time in discussing
this topic as a problem. However, after this thorough
discussion, let me ask you this question:

*DOES YOUR CHURCH SUFFER FROM THE SIN
OF DISOBEDIENCE BY NOT MAKING DISCIPLES?
YES NO*

If you answer yes, Read On!

Reformation Solution # 1:

Clearly, if your church is in the sin of disobedience by refusing to make disciples and leaders of disciples, the need to confess your sin, repent of your sin, and the need to be forgiven of your sin is necessary. Join with your church congregation, pastor(s), and leadership team and as a Body of Christ fall on your knees before God and seek His forgiveness.

In the remainder of this chapter it is my desire to offer you a practical model of discipleship that you can take and apply it to your church to begin the reformation process and hopefully, this will begin the revival process!

A Practical Discipleship Model for Today

A practical model of Christian discipleship for today, can be found in the present day and personal model of Christ United Ministry. Since no churches in the area in which we live are obeying the commandment to make disciples, God called this ministry into existence for His glory. Icenogle states:

> "The small group is a generic form of human community that is trans-cultural, trans-generational and even transcendent. The call to human gathering in groups is a God-created (ontological) and God-directed

(theological) ministry, birthed out of the very nature and purpose of God's being. God as Being exists in community. The natural and simple demonstration of God's communal image for humanity is the gathering of the small group."[168]

Christ United Ministry, founded by my beautiful wife, Vicki and I, is an organism that is dedicated to the glory of Jesus Christ. Christ United Ministry has a website and you can find it at www.christunitedministry.com. It is our desire to become a national network of small group communities to offer many people the opportunity to find the love, care and intimacy of Jesus in, and through, others. As Jesus gave us the best example for discipleship, Christ United Ministry is dedicated to the making of disciples in, and for, Jesus Christ. In this chapter, detailed information on the process of making disciples utilizing the small group format will give clear understanding of the discipleship process in the modern age.

Small Missional Group Format

The model of the small missional group format found in the book of Acts[169] is the model that Christ United Ministry operates as this group addresses every area of a

---

[168] Icenogle. *Biblical Foundations for Small Group Ministry: An Integrational Approach.* 13.
[169] Acts 2: 42 – 47.

person's life by example and word. In the Old Testament, though limited, one can find the use of small missional group format. The small missional group format is found in the area of delegation used by Moses under the guidance of Jethro. In Exodus,[170] one sees clearly the forming of small groups to best serve in a judicial capacity for the interests of man. In the New Testament, Jesus Christ uses the small group format in the choosing and ministry of His twelve disciples and Icenogle makes a powerful statement as he says:

> "The small groups of men and women who responded to, lived with, loved the historical Jesus came together as a new community with the resurrected Christ. They shared His ongoing intimacy with Abba and learned the freedom of intimacy with one another. The gathered men and women came to understand and experience the community of Spirit, in whom the relationship between Jesus and Abba becomes the relationship of human community sharing with Jesus and Abba…Of this ongoing experience of sharing in the Spirit the new community comes to realize that when two or three or more human beings meet with Jesus, they are

---

[170] Exodus 18: 14 – 23.

a microcosm of divine-human community,
an ecclesia."[171]

It is clear in the book of Acts that they met not only in
the temple but also house to house daily as they utilized
the small missional group format. Also, a better example
could not be found for the Christ United Ministry in the
development of disciples than that of the same format
used by Jesus Christ and the Apostles.

The Power of God

Christ United Ministry is always praying and watching
for the power of God the Holy Spirit to draw a person to
Himself through this ministry as we share the love and
gospel of Jesus Christ with others. Jesus makes this point
clearly as He says, "No man can come to me, except the
Father which hath sent me draw him: and I will raise him
up at the last day."[172] God must draw a man to Himself
and under that power of the Holy Spirit that man will be
convicted and stand in the truth. Earley/Dempsey state:

> "As we share the gospel, the Holy Spirit uses
> the Word of God to convince the nonbeliever
> of his sin...He also convinces the nonbeliever
> of righteousness...the Holy Spirit also
> convinces the nonbeliever of judgement...

---

[171] Icenogle. *Biblical Foundations for Small Group Ministry*. 373.
[172] John 6: 44.

> Unless this work occurs, a nonbeliever does not, and cannot, experience salvation."[173]

Once the person who is under conviction confesses he is a sinner and asks Jesus to forgive him of his sins by the blood shed at Calvary, and then he is reborn into the family of God. A person must be reborn into the family of God by their faith in God offered by the blood of Jesus Christ. Paul gives a clear teaching of this process of faith and it is only by faith alone that a man can receive the grace of God to be saved.[174] To grasp the power of a discipleship process, one must first be a disciple. A person cannot become a disciple of Jesus Christ unless they have been reborn by faith. For a man to truly be saved he must possess a true faith in Jesus. According to Herbst, "Faith is being sure of what we hope for and certain of what we do not see (Heb. 11: 1). That literally means that you are so sure of God's power that you live like it is and will be so, regardless of what the circumstances seem to dictate."[175]

The Cost of Discipleship

Once they become brothers or sisters in Christ, they will embark on a lifetime discipleship journey with the goal of being slowly transformed into the likeness of Jesus Christ.

---

[173] Earley, Dave and Rod Dempsey. *Disciple Making Is… 2013. 32.*

[174] Ephesians 2: 8 – 9.

[175] Herbst. *Great Commission Leadership: A workbook on Evangelism, Discipleship and Multiplying Christ-Like Multipliers.* 32.

At Christ United Ministry, it is taken very seriously to discuss, at length, with this person the costs of becoming a disciple of Jesus Christ. Watson and Watson state, "The path to consistent obedience requires a great deal of discipline. Knowledge alone will not get one there."[176] A person must be willing to exercise discipline in their relationship with Jesus Christ if they desire to become a disciple of Jesus. Growth is not based on knowledge but on desire to obey. Smith and Kai say, "In some Christian ministries, we assess how mature a believer is based on how much he knows. But the New Testament assesses the maturity of a believer based on how much he obeys!"[177] There is a cost of discipleship when one accepts and understands their role beginning with obedience. Christ United Ministry teaches that the cost of discipleship in Jesus is simple: It can cost you everything – including your life. Luke quotes Jesus as saying, "So likewise, whosoever he be of you that forsaketh not all that he hath, he cannot be my disciple."[178] A person must be willing to sacrifice his possessions and even his family ties, if needed, to follow Jesus Christ. F.F. Bruce wrote, "The interests of God's kingdom must be paramount with the followers of Jesus, and everything else must take second

---

[176] Watson and Watson. *Contagious Disciple Making: Leading Others on a Journey of Discovery.* 68.

[177] Smith and Kai. *A Discipleship ReRevolution: T4T.* 79.

[178] Luke 14: 33.

place to them, even family ties."[179] Jesus also is quoted as saying, "And He said to them all, If any man will come after me, let him deny himself, and take up his cross daily, and follow me."[180] So a cost to man to become a disciple is that he must deny himself and pick up his cross daily. The denial of self is powerful and difficult for many today. Jesus also says, "And whosoever doth not bear his cross, and come after me, cannot be my disciple."[181] The pursuit of the cross must be the focus of a disciple of Jesus Christ. A person must be willing to deny himself and pick up the cross and follow Jesus Christ. Denial of self is a major issue for people in all ages but especially in the modern era as self seems to reign as god in many people's lives. Koessler explains, "Those who answer the call to discipleship must do so thoughtfully. Christ is not looking for rash decisions that are made in the heat of the moment and then easily abandoned. Those who answer the call must know what Christ requires – He asks for everything."[182] Christ United Ministry stresses to each person to pray and make the commitment to follow Jesus Christ with all of their heart.

---

[179] Bruce, F.F. *The Hard Sayings of Jesus.* Downers Grove, IL: InterVarsity Press. 1983. 119.

[180] Luke 9: 23.

[181] Luke 14: 27.

[182] Koessler, John. *True discipleship: The Art of Following Jesus.* Chicago, IL: Moody Publishers. 2003. 27.

Marks of a Disciple

Also, at Christ United Ministry, growth is imperative for a disciple in Jesus Christ. The teachings of the marks of a disciple are of major emphasis to aid others in their growth. This functions much like a road map so the disciples can ensure they are on the right path and when they find a problem, they can openly discuss it to bring it to resolution. An important point is that discipleship is not a ministry or a program. As Koessler states, "Discipleship is not primarily a matter of what we do. It is an outgrowth of what we are."[183] Well defined marks of growth are an important element to a new disciple as well as to the teachers and leaders of disciples to ensure they are growing in Christ.

One of the first marks of a disciple after they have received salvation is found in the desire and need to be baptized. Jesus Christ commands His disciples to go forth and baptize new believers, as stated in Matthew.[184] Bonhoeffer makes a powerful statement as he says, "The call of Christ and baptism leads Christians into a daily struggle against sin and Satan...The wounds inflicted this way and the scars a Christian carries away from the struggle are living signs of the community of the cross with Jesus."[185] Connecting with Jesus through water

---

[183] Ibid. 12.

[184] Matthew 28: 19.

[185] Bonhoeffer, Dietrich. *Discipleship*. Minneapolis, MN: First Fortress Press. 2003. 88.

baptism helps the new disciple with inward strength and is an outward sign to the world that they have committed their life to Jesus and the struggle. Morris contributes as he states, "Baptism by water also symbolizes the believer's entrance into the sphere of the Holy Spirit."[186] The new disciple is marked by water baptism which shows their decision of accepting the death, burial, and resurrection of Jesus but at the same time it demonstrates the connection to God the Holy Spirit.

The second mark that is carefully watched for in the new disciple is found in the area of obedience. The second major area of the commandment of Jesus is found in Matthew.[187] Jesus is clear as He instructs and commands His disciples to teach new disciples to obey all that Jesus commanded them. Obedience is seen in a devoted relationship with Jesus Christ and the disciple desires to obey their Master, Jesus. Koessler states, "Grace-rooted obedience recognizes that righteousness can only be received as a gift. It cannot be earned as a wage. My obedience is an expression of gratitude for that gift."[188] In love, man has a desire to seek the truth in obedience and seeks forgiveness where he falls short of God's grace.

The third mark of a true disciple is one who is producing fruit as described by Jesus Christ in the book of John.[189]

---

[186] Morris, Leon. *1 Corinthians. Tyndale New Testament Commentaries.* Grand Rapids, MI: Eerdmans. 1958. 174.

[187] Matthew 28: 20.

[188] Koessler. *true discipleship.* 16.

[189] John 15: 7 – 8.

The teaching of the truth that Jesus is the vine and the disciple is the branch is an important lesson. The new disciple receives all that they need from Jesus Christ to produce the fruit that is necessary to bring glory to God. According to Stanford, "In the natural realm, the life that is already complete in the vine is increasingly supplied to the growing branches. The healthy condition of the branches is contingent on their abiding in their position in the vine."[190] One of the most important fruits that a disciple can have produced through them by the Holy Spirit is that of love. It is in the accepting and following of the commandment of Jesus Christ as He says to love others as He has loved you.[191] The condition of the heart of a disciple must be that they are willing to die for this love for others as this is exactly what Jesus ultimately did for them. This love is the last mark that is constantly monitored to ensure the disciple is truly on the right path with Jesus. A disciple must know that God loved them first[192] and then possess the desire to love God and this mark will be shown to the world. If any of the above-mentioned marks are missing or are weak, the disciple is moved to repent in humbleness so God can grow them in this area. Each of these marks demonstrate a loving relationship with Jesus. All fall short of the glory of God and the continual maintenance is imperative for a true

---

[190] Stanford, Miles J. *The Complete Green Letters*. Grand Rapids, MI: Zondervan. 1983. 80.

[191] John 13: 34 – 35.

[192] 1 John 4: 19.

disciple to walk in truth. Koessler states, "Our best hope is to take a good hard look at ourselves and determine which of the marks of discipleship are missing. If having a relationship with Christ is the key to being a true disciple, repentance is always the first step in that relationship."[193] At Christ United Ministry, the disciples are taught to have an inward reflective heart and soul search daily to ensure they are as strong as possible in their relationship with Jesus Christ.

Upward Movement Connection

This ministry is founded on the principles of the Bible with a strong understanding that mankind has great need to be connected to the Head of the church which is Jesus Christ. Earley and Wheeler state, "Our primary purpose is to glorify God and derive our greatest joy from Him. Yet there is more. Not only were we created for God's glory, but we were saved to live for God's glory."[194] This is an Upward Movement. Jesus says this in the Great Commandment, "Thou shalt love the Lord they God with all thy heart, and with all thy soul, and with all thy mind."[195] Man cannot be a disciple for Christ and not possess this true love for God. Benner states, "God's identification with His creation through the incarnation

---

[193] Koessler. *true discipleship*. 24.

[194] Earley and Wheeler. *Evangelism Is…: How to Share Jesus with passion and Confidence*. 13.

[195] Matthew 22: 37.

is the second installment of the Great Love Story…The Son came to reveal the character of the Father. The Son came to bring us back to the Father – back to love."[196] It is God's love for us that draws man to His love for salvation.

Once a person is reborn, they must grow in Christ and this can be done in accordance with His Word, "Then said Jesus to those Jews which believed on Him, If ye continue in my word, then are ye my disciples indeed. And ye shall know the truth, and the truth shall make you free."[197] The disciples must learn the Word of God and grow into His likeness. Whitney says, "No Spiritual Discipline is more important than the intake of God's Word."[198] Also, according to Cole and Helfer, "We believe that knowledge of the Scriptures is a necessary ingredient in the discipleship process."[199] This can be found in the teachings of Paul as the pastor will equip the saints for service[200]. Together the body of Christ is formed and knitted together, and this is found to be on a strong scriptural foundation from His Word.[201] Disciples grow with each other in this process. Earley/Dempsey says, "My job as a disciple maker is to get the new believer into

---

[196] Benner. *Surrender to Love: Discovering the Heart of Christian Spirituality.* 25.

[197] John 8: 31 – 32.

[198] Whitney. *Spiritual Disciplines for The Christian Life.* 28.

[199] Cole and Helfer. *Church Transfusion: Changing Your Church Organically from the Inside Out.* 130.

[200] Ephesians 4: 12.

[201] Ephesians 4: 16.

an environment of mutual accountability and learning under the Word of God."[202]

Inward Movement Connection

A disciple then must be connected to each of his/her brothers and sisters in Christ. Putman says, "An important value that needs to be supported and protected in our churches is relationship – relationship with the true God and relationship among believers. The church needs relationship, not just because it is the best way to teach, but because our relationships are the evidence that what we preach is true."[203] The next step is how the disciple must look inward. This is the Inward Movement and founded on the Scripture in His Word as Jesus says, "And the second is like unto it, thou shalt love thy neighbor as thyself."[204] To love God is to be in an obedient relationship with Him and to love your neighbor is to be in relationship with them also. Ortberg states, "God uses people to form people…we are rooted and our souls are nourished in the love of God and other people."[205] Relationship with God and with God's people is the key to love and growth.

---

[202] Earley, Dave and Rod Dempsey. *Disciple Making Is… 2013. 149.*

[203] Putman. *real-life discipleship: building churches that make disciples.* 50.

[204] Matthew 22: 39.

[205] Ortberg. *The me I want to be: becoming God's best version of you.* 182 – 183.

Outward Movement Connection

Disciples must then be on mission with God and go seeking the lost. Again, love is the central theme here and this is the Outward Movement. Jesus gives a new commandment to His disciples as He says, "A new commandment I give unto you, That ye love one another, as I have loved you, that ye also love one another. By this shall all men know that ye are my disciples, if ye have love one to another."[206] A disciple of Christ must carry this love for the lost in his heart. Luke is recorded saying, "For the Son of man is come to seek and to save that which was lost."[207] A disciple of Jesus Christ should desire to imitate his Master, obey, and follow in His footsteps in seeking those who are lost and help them connect to the person of Jesus Christ. This is really the essence of Love. Clegg and Bird make an eloquent statement, "The essence of God's mission is extravagant love…The essence of God's love is to make a difference, by God's power, in the lives of other people, for now and for eternity."[208] When all of the movements, Upward - Inward - and Outward are being exercised within the small group format of community, it is my belief that the model of Jesus and the apostles is being followed and God will bless as He does in the Bible.

---

[206] John 13: 34.

[207] Luke 19: 10.

[208] T. Clegg and T. Bird. *Lost in America*. Loveland, CO: Group Publishing. 2001. 20.

Multiplication Movement Connection

The disciples participate together with others in the worshipping, fellowshipping, sharing of meals, communion, baptisms, devotions, Bible teachings, community outreach, and missions. This is the overall Christian discipleship process found at Christ United Ministry. Christ United Ministry always has her eyes open for God to reveal new leaders that God is building and creating for His glory. Wilkes says, "Leadership begins when a God-revealed mission captures a person. This person turns leader as he becomes servant to the mission."[209] The ultimate goal of Christ United Ministry is found in God's principles of the multiplication movement connection and that is to build new leaders to send out and make more disciples and this is found in accordance with the Scriptures. Smith and Kai say it simply, "Leadership multiplication is the engine the Spirit uses to sustain a movement." [210] This is a Biblical principle that many miss in today's world. If one will look closely at the example of Jesus Christ in His discipleship process, He began with twelve disciples and as He grew them up - sent eleven of them out - under the power of the Holy Spirit - they changed the world. The multiplication process was in effect and this is the true way that disciples of today need to focus the churches attention. The world is growing

---

[209] Wilkes. *Jesus On Leadership: Discovering the secrets of servant leadership.* 19.
[210] Smith and Kai. *T4T: A Discipleship ReRevolution.* 281.

exponentially, and the church is failing. If there is a desire to catch up and bring glory to God, the multiplication process is the only way.

Obedience

Lastly, Christ United Ministry is built on the obedience to the commandment found in Matthew 28: 19 - 20..."Go ye therefore and teach all nations, baptizing them in the name of the Father, and of the Son, and of the Holy Ghost: Teaching them to observe all things whatsoever I have commanded you: and, lo, I am with you alway, even unto the end of the world. Amen." Obedience to all the commandments of God is essential to the journey with God. Earley and Dempsey state, "God demands absolute obedience to His commands."[211] Jesus also says in John 14: 15, "If you love Me, you will keep My commandments." As many today only give lip service to the commandments, Christ United Ministry is focused on the need to be obedient to God to receive the full blessings of God.

---

[211] Earley and Dempsey. *Disciple Making Is…: How to Live the Great Commission with Passion and Confidence.* 50.

Chapter 8

Organization vs. Organism: A Leadership Issue

"For as the body is one, and hath many
members, and all the members
of that one body, being many, are
one body: so also, is Christ."
1 Corinthians 12: 12

Church problem # 2:

First, let me discuss the need for reformation in the managing of God's Church. Man loves to take control and ownership of things that are not his. Look at our government – I will say no more. God's Church is first a body of His Son, The Body of Christ! This means that the church first and foremost must be operated like a body. An organism is much different than an organization. If you want to run a Boys Club that is great, and it needs to be run like an organization. God's church is a body and deserves the respect and honor to be operated like an organism. Cole states, "Running a church like a business, however, will suck the life out of the church. The church will die..."[212]

I like to illustrate that point like this: The **Heart** of the church is Jesus Christ. The **Spirit** of the church is God the Holy Spirit. The **Soul** of the church are the people of God who have been reborn, and their souls have been restored by the power of God through the salvation process. The **Hands and Feet** of the church are the people on God's mission "Going" into their communities extending the love of Jesus to everyone by serving them and not judging them. The **Breath** from the Lungs of the church are the new converts – new disciples - that have been brought into the precious relationship with God through Christ through the evangelism efforts of discipleship.

I once was the pastor of a church in the Cumberland Presbyterian Denomination in Arkansas. At a board meeting with the elders, I began the meeting by offering an empty seat at the table. I informed the elders that it was my belief that Jesus should have a seat, since it was truly His church and we should honor that. I will never forget the look on the faces of these people after I said these words. It was like they were looking at me like, this guy is crazy. They had little, if any, clue to what I was offering. Let me be brutally honest on this point, this

---

[212] Cole, Neil. *Organic Leadership: Leading Naturally Right Where You Are.* Grand Rapids, MI: Baker Publishing Group. 2009. 121.

board of elders didn't want Jesus Christ in His church and I suspect that is the truth in many churches across America. If you ask one hundred leaders who runs their church, 99 would say God, but the truth, only one or two churches are operated by the power of the Holy Spirit. Man runs the organization of the church and they don't want God involved. Scazzero states, "The overall health of any church or ministry depends primarily on the emotional and spiritual health of its leadership."[213] Again, being honest, God would run His church as an organic body - an organism, so how can God be running the church when it is run like an organization. The truth is, if you are not running your church like an organism then God is not involved in your church, *PERIOD*!

Later, Vicki and I resigned from this church when we learned how they were in sin because they ran the church like an organization. This is a story I will never forget, and it is my desire to drive this point home. First, one person would count the money collected from the Sunday service. She would then inform the board of elders of the total amount and wait for guidance. The board of elders had an agreement to give back to the Arkansas Presbytery 10% of all monies collected by the church. This board decided that they didn't like this agreement, so they had other plans. They opened two checking accounts in the name of the church. If anyone investigated them, they

---

[213] Scazzero, Peter. *The Emotionally Healthy Church: A Strategy for Discipleship that Actually Changes Lives.* Grand Rapids, MI: Zondervan. 2010. 20.

would see they paid their dues in accordance with the agreement. However, and watch this, if they collected $1,000.00 on a Sunday morning, they would report that they only received $100.00. They would send a check for $10.00 to the Arkansas Presbytery and no one would be the wiser. Then secondly, they would then take the other $890.00 ($1,000 – $100 = $900 – $10 (presbytery fee) = $890.00) and deposit this in their second "secret" account. They would then spend it in ways they felt they wanted to such as to remodel parts of the building or, and this is so bold, extend personal loans to other elders on the board. When I questioned them on this, I made my point by asking how many loans they extended to any congregational members of the church. Did they offer anyone other than a board member a loan? The answer was NO! This statement of fact on this board isn't a personal indictment on any of them personally, but only a weakness exposed of one board, on how they fall to sin when they are running the church like an organization and not like an organism. This is how a church is run like an organization and this is one of the needs that church must accept, reformation.

Another area of weakness in a church that is run by a board when they operate like an organization can be found in the selection of a pastor. This is a major issue for all churches as most churches want the most for their buck. They are going to pay this man (or woman in some cases) a very nice salary along with a house, expenses and benefits so they want the best person for their money. Most churches establish a pastor search committee, beg for prayers from the congregation for this committee, and then leave the search up to the committee. Most pastor search committees profess that they hope God would send them their pastor. However, I will tell you that almost every pastor search committee who is waiting on God's man, also decides to take control of the operation and amazingly, poof! There is their pastor! It is amazing how that happens. Well, the truth of this is that God isn't involved and the committee got exactly what they wanted in their efforts and they are always the most shocked people when that man turns out to be a criminal or just one that didn't live up to their expectations.

Here is a recent example of this process. My wife and I were driving to visit a church one of our friends attend called Mt. Zion Baptist Church in South Side, Arkansas. We were excited to just go and worship God together with our friend and meet some new friends. On the way to his church, my wife googled the name of another church and the website said they had a need for a youth pastor. I have a heart for any flock that is without a senior or youth pastor. I always see the sheep in a field, unprotected and without guidance, and that breaks my heart. Vicki and I both felt the leading of the Holy Spirit to change direction and we headed to another Baptist Church in rural Arkansas. No doubt God has sent us to this church – why God sent us was a mystery.

The first moment we walked into this church it was a pleasure. The people were so friendly and open. Unlike the other Baptist Church where we experienced not one "good morning," this group of people fell all over us. We both felt like it was one of the warmest and friendliest churches we had ever been too. That would change!

We sat in a Sunday School class and we met a special lady. She was one of the sweetest ladies I had ever met. We had a great discussion on Genesis 1: 26-27 and it was so inspiring. Vicki was so excited when I got my Master of Divinity degree and then when I got my Doctor of Ministry degree; she was so proud. She would tell everyone what we had accomplished and always with God's blessings. We quickly learned how people pushed back and are intimidated by others being successful. You would think that people would be excited and happy to have someone in class with that type of education so you could glean from them and maybe learn some things, but that wasn't the case. Because people can be so rude, Vicki and I decided to no longer tell anyone about our academic accomplishments. We didn't tell anyone in this church of our background.

We were so happy God had led us to this church and thought maybe this would be the church where we could worship and serve God. Well, later that morning in the Sunday service, we learned that they not only needed a youth pastor but also a senior pastor. My heart broke for them as I discussed their needs and I never asked what happened to the last pastor. It just wasn't important to me. I was just moved to serve God by serving them. I would just say how sorry I was for their loss and would be in prayer for God to be glorified by bringing His pastor to them. I was just moved to serve God by serving them.

A few days past and I had been in prayer for this church and I felt God's calling on me to offer my help and assistance to them. Let me be open and honest – I am not a called pastor – I am a called shepherd. I have no desire to run, or be in charge, of a church, but I am called like the Holy Spirit is sent to come along side and to guide, love, and protect a flock so they can flourish and grow until God blesses that church with a pastor. Here is a sad statement on this church.

We never got the chance to even explain this to this church. I placed my resume' and academic accomplishments in a manila envelope and went to a person that I could tell was an important person of the church. I wasn't sure if he was a deacon or leader but one that everyone loved and would listen too. I gave him my envelope and told him to keep this confidential. I asked him to give these documents to the deacons/pastor search committee but not to tell anyone who I was or the title I carry. He agreed and I left it right there with one exception.

I was completing my graduate degree in counseling and had to complete the last class called an internship. I had asked a person from the local association office in

Arkansas, if I could do my internship for this counseling program. They agreed and I met and asked a lady who was doing biblical counseling for the same association to be my supervisor and she agreed, and I thought everything was good.

I went to this person of the association and asked him to put in a good word to this church leadership to support me in shepherding this church until they find a pastor. He laughed and said, "They just called me and asked me to preach Sunday." He then said he didn't know if he was even going to preach. I asked him to let me know either way and informed him that I was interested to preach if he chose not to preach. He said he would call me and let me know his decision. He Never Did! Was I lied to again? Not by a man of God – Really?

Vicki and I attended this Baptist church on the following Sunday morning and sure enough, this person was preaching. He never called me, and I've wondered if church politics was kicking in! The people became very cold and distant, even more than the previous time we attended. I knew something was up. Could it be church politics? Now, mind you, Vicki and I never spoke to anyone to share our desire to serve or anything about our backgrounds. I approached one of the women that had been selected to serve on the pastor search committee and asked her if they had received my application. She rudely looked at me and said, "Yes." I informed her that I thought she should put that application on hold and she abruptly said, "I will inform the committee." She didn't say, Oh I'm so sorry, can I offer any help to you on this decision? She didn't say, Oh I'm so sorry to hear that, but I will let the committee know to put it on hold. Nope – she coldly and rudely stated "I will let the committee know!" She turned and walked away! I knew the fix was in! I knew the leadership of the association and this church had been compromised and the rejection process was in place!

If I could offer one passage of scripture to the many people of leadership of the church, (and pay close attention to the words, not all Christians, and not all the people of the church, but the many people of the church that operate the church for your own power and position: Jesus made this passage of scripture) and it is the saddest scripture in the Bible: "Not every one that saith unto me, Lord, Lord, shall enter into the kingdom of heaven; but he that doeth the will of my Father which is in heaven. Many will say to me in that day, Lord, Lord, have we not prophesied in thy name? and in thy name have cast out devils? And in thy name done many wonderful works? And then will I profess unto them, I never knew you: depart from me, ye that work iniquity."[214] Look closely, these people were working for Christ, or so they thought. In the reality of their mind, they thought they were serving Jesus, but they were serving themselves. This, for me, is why it is one of the saddest passages of scripture as it stands against men

---

[214] Matthew 7: 21-23

and women who use Jesus Christ for *their* gain but in the end – it is their eternal loss. Also, how many people must suffer under their polluted and compromised leadership?

As I speak of this issue, remember I am not speaking of the average person who attends church faithfully and is a member of a church. I am speaking of the corrupted and compromised leadership of the local church. My wife and I miss the members of the congregation of the church we pastored, but we had to separate from them so as not to cause harm to them. If they had known the truth about how their money was being used for things that weren't bringing glory to God by the leadership of their church, they would have left the church. It wasn't my desire to hurt them. It is not my desire to hurt the body of Christ. We desire to work with men and women of leadership that want to serve God by serving others in a Biblical way. We miss many of the congregation of the many churches we had the pleasure of worshipping God with, but we always found the problems that are killing the church are lodged in the leadership of the church. (Now, I will address one problem the congregation of a dying church has but that will be in a later time in this chapter.)

DOES YOUR CHURCH SUFFER FROM ORGANIZATION LEADERSHIP AND NOT ORGANISM LEADERSHIP? YES NO

If yes, then your church is suffering and needs reformation and change. Read On!

The Reformation Solution # 2:

Every church board that isn't running God's church like an organism must ask the congregation to join them and move to their knees and confess the sin of running God's church like an organization. The above story about the church board isn't an indictment on every church but only shows the temptations that are offered when a church isn't operating the church like an organism. The congregation must be loving and moved to forgive the board and together make a commitment to God and each other to change the course of doing business and leave a seat at the board table for Jesus. A point on this issue must be made at this time. Congregations of churches *MUST* become engaged in the business of the church and *NOT* just let leadership of their churches operate without a checks and balances system. No one is perfect and Satan will slip into your church and turn very good men and women from the truth to a lie. Stand up *WITH* your leadership and hold them accountable for their actions and this will help them remain focused on their work for Christ. One possible way to change the operation is to have one representative of the congregation to join the board only as an observer. Allow them to record all business and make any objections that are necessary and report back to the congregation. If you need this area of reformation in your church, gather in humbleness to God and ask the Holy Spirit to offer you other solutions that would best bring glory to God and blessings to your church.

Chapter 9

False Teachers and Preachers (Pastors)

"Beware of false prophets, which come to you in
sheep's clothing, but inwardly they are ravening
wolves. You shall know them by their fruits."
Matthew 7: 15

Church Problem # 3:

(Artist and Author Unknown)

Now we arrive at possibly the most difficult issue found in the church. If you thought the last section on leadership in the church was rough, prepare yourself for a journey. I love the above scripture because this is an indictment of our times and the condition of the church. It was true in the times of the Old Testament, it was true during the times of Jesus on this earth, and it is true today. Many of our churches are led by men and women that have no idea what a calling is on their life to be the pastor of a church. It is my opinion, but I believe that many pastors today have selected the business of religion as it pays well and offers wonderful benefits such as a house, all expenses paid, and a good retirement plan. It isn't the best, but for what a man must do, he can pull this off easily. I also believe that many pastors are good people who think they are called by God, but they are just good people who have a desire to help others. They have convinced themselves that there is a call on their lives because they need that, but that doesn't make it a call from God on their life to lead the church.

This is a serious problem for the church. The church acts as if everyone that crosses their path and says that they have a call on their life to pastor a church is being truthful. It isn't a truth – this is how Satan infiltrates the Church of America and begins to lead her down a path of destruction. This is one of the reasons the church is dying as secularism and liberalism has permeated the church.

The church is sacred, and a place of worship and man

has chosen to operate it like the organization we spoke of earlier and Satan has slipped behind the pulpit with a charming and sweet personality and a cute smile. There is an old saying, "If you are looking for Satan, don't forget to look behind the pulpit in a church!" Most of the pastors today state they are led by the Holy Spirit and are called by God to pastor the church.

Isn't it so arrogant of a group of leaders to act like they are led by the Holy Spirit, only to succumb to the politics of this group and hire a friend or a person they know even though there are better candidates available? This is man taking authority over God. I believe that the Bible says the wages of sin is death!

I have met only one leader of a church that was acting as a pastor that honestly said outright that he was not called by God. Every pastor I have met and discussed this issue with has claimed they were called by God. If that were true, why is the church broken and in a death spiral? Why, as we have demonstrated in previous chapters in this book, are these *CALLED* men of God not in obedience to the commandments of God? Why is the church not evangelizing their communities and producing a pile of new saved converts for their churches? Why is the church not producing disciples and more importantly, not producing leaders of disciples? I submit that *NOT* all men are called of God.

Before we get too deep into this subject, let me tell you that I can hear tens of thousands of church going people right now saying, "Oh, we love our pastor, he preaches and teaches us, he is always on call for us when we are sick and he is such a wonderful man....*WE LOVE OUR PASTOR!*" I've had this conversation with several people that attended a church in Mt. Pleasant, Arkansas. Many said that exact statement that I wrote above. Now, if you can set your pride aside and try not to be offended by this, maybe you will glean from this what God wants you to know.

The pastor of this church does preach something, usually a nice sermon about a story in the Bible. When he preaches, and I've heard him preach, I've never heard him *PREACH THE GOSPEL OF JESUS CHRIST.* He never called man to confession and repentance for their sins and never taught them about how God will forgive them of their sins if they will confess and repent (1 John 1: 9). I never saw any person come down the aisle and give their life to Christ in the humble act of surrender and receiving Jesus Christ as their Lord and Savior. Now, I will wait as you get your calculator and begin the process if calculating the large number of people that have walked the aisle in your church. Go ahead as I wait for you. Do you even need a calculator? The number is very small isn't it? So, if this is true in your church, your pastor is one of the problems. If he is truly called by God to preach the gospel of Jesus Christ, your church would be experiencing a much larger response to God's message of Jesus Christ and the plan of salvation.

> "For I am not ashamed of the gospel of Christ:
> for it is the power of God unto salvation to
> everyone that believeth; to the Jew first, and
> also to the Greek." Romans 1: 16

Clearly, it is the gospel of Jesus Christ that has the power to bring people to the plan of salvation but if your pastor isn't preaching it, then your church will not be experiencing the power of the Holy Spirit in your church.

Allow me to interject this message at this point. There is a difference between the gospel of Jesus Christ and the *FULL* gospel of Jesus Christ. The gospel of Jesus Christ is the *good news* that Jesus Christ was sent out of heaven by His Father and took on the image of man, preached love and truth, was crucified, shedding His blood so we, mankind, could find the path to heaven through the forgiveness of our sins found only in His blood. Let me ask you this question – Have you ever met the Person of Jesus Christ? Most churches don't teach this point – we *MUST* have a response to the good news of Jesus Christ. How we respond reflects the true condition of our heart. This is where many preachers fall short. They simply say you need to be forgiven of sin and ask Jesus into your heart and you are saved. This is *FALSE*! We *MUST* confess we are a sinner in need of a Savior! We *MUST* confess we have had another god before God and his name was Self. We *MUST* kneel before God in humbleness that He is our true God and our sin has separated us from Him until now. We *MUST* then repent (turn from the sin and turn to God) and this is an absolute. Once we do this before Him, we invite the Person of Jesus Christ into our hearts and submit to His will and ask Him to live in our hearts. As it says in 1 John 1: 9, "If you confess your sins before me, I am faithful to forgive you and cleanse you of all unrighteousness." God will forgive you of your sins and the Holy Spirit will move into your heart sealing your salvation for eternity.

There *MUST* be change. The Bible speaks of the old creature dying and once there is a re-birth, there is a *NEW CREATURE*! If you *are* a new creature – you will then *be* a new creature. You will experience a *CHANGE*! Many people experience a "feel good" moment with God and feel like they are reborn but never experience a change of heart. If this is you, please re-read the above section and humble yourself before the one true God and find your peace and path to eternal security. This is what is needed in our churches today! This is what *MUST* be preached in our churches today!

Back to the story! The people that attend the church we were discussing are very religious people. They do like their liturgical ceremonies as they appear very Catholic in their ways of the religious process on Sunday Morning. However, their process isn't a problem for me. How many true disciples is this pastor (and his church) responsible for making in their church? The acceptance of salvation is the beginning of the discipleship process so if you really didn't need your calculator for the understanding of only a few people accepting Jesus Christ in your church, you have a small number of new converts that can qualify as disciples. I once was asked by the board of a church I had pastored, "why do you preach on salvation so much because we are all saved at this church?" Really? Can you believe a statement was made like that? Later that year one of this elder's dear friends gave his life to Christ and I have always wondered, what did that event do to the hearts of those in that church who agreed with the above statement of them all being saved. I hope it drove them closer to God to address their own salvations. So, if your church is all saved, then how is the level of discipleship in your church?

If there is a great deal of making of disciples, your church would reflect this. Your church would be on mission every day seeking the lost in your community and performing many acts of kindness to others to help draw them closer to Christ for salvation. Is that happening at your church? You love this pastor, but he is not making disciples, he is not teaching you how to love God by loving others, and he is not preaching the gospel of Jesus Christ, but you hold to loving this man as your pastor. Can you at least see how this would fly in the face of God? Who are you more worried of offending, God or man? Pastors, this goes for you also! People, please don't hold to loving your leaders who are not serving God by serving you. If they are not doing this, it is time to close the doors or work with this person on confession, repentance and obedience to serve God. Allow me to share another story.

Vicki and I were sitting in a non-denominational church not far from our house in Arkansas. I had entered a superficial relationship with this so-called pastor who disagreed with the definition we have offered of a disciple. He also told me that he disagreed with my findings on the church not making disciples and offered for us to agree to disagree. I must tell you that this man had zero theological education and/or training and I'm not sure, but I didn't remember if he was even ordained minister, though he may have had one attribute. Here is a man who is uneducated and untrained fighting me on data that he had no idea of how to discredit and offered him several times to do so. He wouldn't and he couldn't. He did come to me and ask me to teach a section to his church on a Wednesday night service and I agreed. He said he would handle the discipleship training if I would handle another area of concern. I almost fell out laughing in his face as here is a man with zero clue, in the company of a highly trained man (not to boast), and he wouldn't allow me to teach a subject that I received my doctorate. Allow me to give you an example; a surgeon discusses the surgical procedures with an untrained man, then the untrained man offers to the surgeon that he can teach a class on giving a shot when the untrained man would teach on the delicate intricacies of brain surgery! This was one for the books.

This man began to preach one Sunday morning, and Vicki and I was in attendance and - *WAIT FOR IT* – he began to explain how Satan doesn't really hate you and that was a theory that has been taken out of context in the Bible. We left! Really? Is this a called man of God preaching the Word of God? I must say, I don't really think that this type of person is out of step with many churches in America. My fear is that many churches would probably think he was being truthful about being called since they would have little, if any, idea what a called pastor would look like.

DOES YOUR CHURCH SUFFER FROM FALSE PREACHERS/TEACHERS? YES NO
If yes, your church is suffering and needs reformation and change. Read On!

Reformation Solution # 3:

Priority # 1 of a Called Man of God – This man who claims he is called of God ***MUST BE CALLED OF GOD.*** There are many men and women who are pretenders and are only looking for a job. The call of God is unmistakable and unshakable. A man who isn't called, but pretending, will ultimately fold under the pressure of the role of pastor if he isn't called by God. Now don't get me wrong, a pretender of a call matched with an ungodly church will work out fine and may even grow in numbers. However, I believe God will always stand against a pretender.

> "If anyone sets his heart on being an overseer, he desires a noble task. Now the overseer must be above reproach, the husband of one wife, temperate, self-controlled, respectable, hospitable, able to teach, not given to drunkenness, not violent but gentle, not quarrelsome, not a love of money. He must mange his own family well and see that his children obey him with proper respect. If anyone does not know how to mange his own family, how can he take care of God's church? He must not be a recent convert, or he may become conceited and fall under the same judgment as the devil. He must also have a good reputation with outsiders, so that he will not fall into disgrace and into the devil's trap." 1 Timothy 3: 1-7

A man who isn't called by God will have great trouble in adhering to all the requirements that God gave to Paul to set forth for a called pastor. I would think that any church looking for a pastor would be holding this scripture up as a measuring stick and not be moved to hire anyone that doesn't meet these standards. I wonder how many churches in America don't bother holding to that scripture when hiring a pastor? I knew of another local church in Arkansas that didn't hold this scripture as their measuring stick. If they had used this requirement that a called man of God must be able to teach, they would have never hired this pastor. He fit their requirement, not God's requirement – *HE WAS LOCAL AND THEY KNEW HIM! BOOM*! Isn't that a disgrace and it flies in the face of God! That causes me to be filled with righteous anger.

I return to the story about the Baptist Church who was without a senior pastor and had developed their search committee, I must share this story with you. You have just read probably the most used passage of scripture for the requirements of a *CALLED* pastor. Vicki and I were sitting in the last Sunday sermon that we will ever attend at that church and it concluded and we were heading out when a man raised his voice and said, "Oh, I almost forgot, pick up a survey sheet and fill it out and tell us what you want in a pastor." I looked at Vicki and about dropped to my knees. Really? God's Word on the subject is clear! This so-called search committee is asking for suggestions on what a congregation wants in a pastor. I couldn't even pick up a form and read it as I was fearful of what I would put in my mind. I could only think it must have questions like: Do you want a handsome man? Do you prefer a handsome woman? How tall do you want a pastor? Should he/she have dreamy deep blue eyes? I just couldn't give in to read this survey. I looked at Vicki and said, how about a *CALLED MAN OF GOD WHO IS SENT BY GOD TO YOU*! Not good enough? Amazing isn't it!

The called man of God *must* make sure of his calling to bring glory to God and blessings to him and his family.

> "Therefore, my brothers, be all the more eager to make your calling and election sure. For if you do these things, you will never fall, and you will receive a rich welcome into the eternal kingdom of our Lord and Savior Jesus Christ." 1 Peter 1: 10-11 (NIV)

Priority # 2 of a Called Man of God – He must **preach the gospel of Jesus Christ**. Many preachers don't even have a clue what the gospel of Jesus Christ is today. That is the most important priority of a preacher – *PREACH THE GOSPEL OF JESUS CHRIST*:

> "For though I preach the gospel, I have nothing to glory of: for necessity is laid upon me; yea, woe is unto me, if I preach not the gospel!" 1 Corinthians 9: 16

Man is called by God to preach the gospel and is cursed if he doesn't preach the gospel of Jesus Christ. Could this be another reason the American Church is dying? Is there a curse on our men and women who are preaching in churches and preaching nonsense like Satan doesn't hate you but should be preaching the gospel of Jesus Christ?

Priority # 3 of a Called Man of God – He must be a **teacher of the Word of God** to edify and grow up his flock into the likeness of Jesus Christ.

> "Not many of you should presume to be teachers, my brothers, because you know that we who teach will be judged more strictly."
> James 3: 1 (NIV)

We who are called must be willing and able to teach the Word of God to others. Those who are not called by God, though they may be knowledgeable in the Word, should be very careful about teaching, or do they not know they will be judged much more harshly than others? We have many teachers out there that do not know this scripture and probably don't really care. Teaching is one of the most fundamental responsibilities of a called man of God.

Vicki and I sat in a Baptist Church close to our home in Arkansas and this preacher, who was an associate pastor of the church, was teaching a class from the book of Acts. You are not going to believe this, but he began to teach that Paul was the thirteenth called apostle of Jesus Christ. My mouth dropped open and I was stunned. I mean, I can understand a man making a mistake but to teach this was total nonsense. He didn't just make one statement about this subject; he was trying to convince the congregation of this as a fact. If that wasn't sad enough, the senior pastor was sitting in the congregation that Sunday and I kept looking at him to see if he would correct this man.

I was so upset I went to him after the service as he was standing next to the pastor and I confronted him. I asked him if he knew of a man named Mathias. He said no and I said, well, Mathias was the thirteenth man and he was elected to fill the spot of Judas after his death. I'm not sure he even knew who Judas was. This man, if you can believe this story, eventually was hired by a local church in Arkansas as Senior Pastor. Prior to this hiring, I had met one of the wives of a prominent man of that church and we began to discuss their need for a pastor. She complained that she was getting resumes from all over the country. I asked her why was that a problem and she said that she knew that they only wanted to hire a local man that they knew and wouldn't consider anyone else. Now that church is led by the Holy Spirit and they hired a man who says he is called of God but doesn't know who replaced Judas as an apostle. What else does this man *teach* that isn't in the Bible? What else does this man *preach* that isn't in the Bible? The scary thing is that no one questioned that pastor that day and I was the only one to approach him. I guess that is an indictment on the church, huh?

Priority # 4 of a Called Man of God – Now this is one area that I have selected as one of my personal best and favorites. I feel that every called man of God should possess two educational levels of accomplishment: first, he

MUST have received at least a Master of Divinity Degree and preferably a Doctor of Ministry Degree, and second, he *MUST* hold a Master of Pastoral Counseling Degree. The first area of accomplishment is obvious, and all called men of God should have and hold a degree in higher education. *PERIOD*! Anyone who opposes this position is probably a person who wants a job but didn't dedicate himself to learning all he can about God and how to love God and love others! The second area, and I won't speak long on this issue but one of the greatest failures of the church, in my humble opinion, is when we let the pastors of our churches direct the flock that God has given them, to secular counselors. A person in pain and going through life's trials and tribulations will seek counsel in hopes of getting out of pain. One of the first people they would choose is their spiritual leader. However, most pastors have little, or no training in this field, so they make an excuse as to why they can't do anything and send their flock to a secular counselor or psychotherapist. This will fill their minds and hearts with worldly teachings and many times also to medication. This was never God's plan and we should be ashamed that we have allowed this to occur. If the "search" committees in our churches truly cared about their search for a called man of God, they would hold to three requirements:

1. All of God's requirements found in 1 Timothy 3: 1 – 7

2. A called man of God who has received the proper academic level of study
3. A called man of God who has received his Master of Pastoral Counseling Degree

Priority # 5 of a Called Man of God – This is the final in my list of priorities for a called man of God to pastor a church. This man must possess the understanding of the failures in and of the church in two major areas. The first area is in obeying the commandment of Jesus Christ:

> "A new commandment I give unto you, that ye love one another; as I have loved you, that ye also love one another. By this shall all men know that ye are my disciples, if ye have love one to another." John 13: 34 – 35

The leader of a Christian Church in America *MUST* possess the heart of a person who knows love, which means he must know God. If he is called by God, he will be connected to God and connected to *LOVE*! If this man knows God and knows love, he will be moved to teach you and I about this *LOVE*. He will be compelled to teach and show love to others. He will be best adapted to show love more than to talk about love. As Jesus Christ said in this scripture, first we are commanded to love others and, second, the world will know we are His disciples. If we know love, we will be making disciples and then we will be making leaders of disciples. We then will not only *BE THE CHURCH;* we will be His disciples on mission making disciples! *BOOM*! This called man of God must be a disciple maker!

Chapter 10

Evangelical Outreach to Your Community

"A new commandment I give unto you, that ye love one another; as I have loved you, that ye also love one another. By this shall all men know that ye are my disciples, if ye have love one to another."
John 13: 34-35

Church Problem # 4:

Clearly, Jesus teaches us and commands us to love others as He loved us. When we do love others with the love of Christ – the world knows we are disciples. I challenge you to reach out to others with His love and begin to make disciples and show the world that you are a disciple of Jesus Christ. Cole states:

> "Christianity is always just one generation away from extinction. If we fail to reproduce ourselves and pass the torch of life to the

next generation, Christianity will be over in just one generation. Yet, because of the power of multiplication, we are also just one generation away from worldwide fulfillment of the Great Commission – the choice is ours."[215]

We must understand that if we love others, we must make disciples and more importantly, make leaders of disciples so we can use the Godly principle of multiplication. This is the love that Jesus Christ gave us as our template to bring glory to God.

This is a major problem and also a sin, as stated earlier in this book. The American Church refuses to participate in the making of disciples and therefore, shows the world that not only are we in disobedience to our Lord and Savior, we are also not disciples ourselves. If we are to find the path back into the Will of God and reconcile with God, we must confess, repent, and seek forgiveness of God. We can never find revival for our church if we stand against the truth of God.

Is your church penetrating the community, Monday – Saturday, in a small missional group format organized to extend love to others in the community in a systematic and organized manner? We have lost the evangelical desires to share the gospel of Jesus Christ as a corporate body. I

---

[215] Cole, Neil. *Organic Leadership: Leading Naturally right Where You Are.* Grand Rapids, MI: Baker Books Publishing Group. 2009. 278.

believe this is one of the effects that comes directly from the leadership operating the church as an organization instead of an organism. Evangelism is man's desire to reach others in the community and share love with them. When a church is evangelizing their community in a systematic and organized manner, they are sharing the love of Christ by example and telling the world that they love them. The key to evangelism is found in Matthew 28: 19 in the first word, "*GO.*" We must be *going* into the world and sharing love to reach the lost. Some ideas of this effort is a daily feeding outreach, a daily ministry to the elderly, a daily offering of pastoral counseling services, a daily outreach to the poor, or a daily prayer walk to share the love of Christ with others. These are but a few things a church can do to extend love to others so that they can begin a relationship with you. They will be moved by you before they are ever moved to accept Jesus Christ. We teach, you must show the love of Christ by example before you share the love of Christ in the Word. Small missional groups are great to facilitate the gathering of Christians with non-believers in a common event like a cooking club. People who are not connected to God through Christ will grow to love you and then you will be able to introduce them to Christ. These are some of the ways we must love others and show the world we are His disciples.

I will explain more about how to accomplish this task in the reformation solution explanation.

IS YOUR CHURCH SUFFERING FROM THE LACK OF EVANGELICAL OUTREACH TO YOUR COMMUNITY? YES NO

If yes, your church is suffering and needs reformation and change. Read On!

Reformation Solution # 4:

How do we teach others to love God, self, and others? This seems a monumental task and may be a contributing factor why the American Church has suffered so greatly in the end times. However, if we don't change through reformation, we cannot bring glory to God and blessings to our selves and others.

Priority Solution # 1 – We must examine our hearts individually to seek the truth. Are we really connected to God through Christ Jesus? Have we truly accepted the truth about our own heart conditions? I think one of the most important steps in this process is to open our hearts and minds to God the Holy Spirit and allow Him to reveal to us the truth concerning our condition. Some of you may be thinking, I know I'm saved so I don't need to take step one. Allow me to share this fact: If everyone who professes Jesus as their Lord was truly saved, why are we in the mess we are in today? Without question, there is a wiring problem in some people, so I am just offering to you a chance to ensure you have accepted Jesus Christ as your *Lord* and Savior. True confession and repentance are the only way to the throne of God, and it cuts right through the person of Jesus Christ who said:

> "...I am the way, the truth, and the life, no man cometh unto the Father, but by me."
> John 14: 6

The possible second disconnect in this process is between those who profess Jesus Christ as their Lord and Savior and the true surrender of their souls to their Creator. In short, a person cannot be a disciple of Jesus Christ if they have not been reborn in Christ. Earley and Wheeler state, "Effective evangelism introduces unbelievers to a relationship with Jesus."[216] They must have their souls restored into the image of God through confession and repentance. Once this has occurred, the person must surrender completely to Christ. This is the determining factor between a follower of Christ and a disciple of Christ.

> "I beseech you therefore brethren, by the mercies of God that ye present your bodies a living sacrifice, holy, acceptable unto God, which is your reasonable service. And be not conformed to this world: but be ye transformed by the renewing of your mind that ye may prove what is that good,

---

[216] Earley, Dave and David Wheeler. *Evangelism Is...: How to Share Jesus with passion and Confidence.* Nashville, TN: B&H Academic Publishing Group. 2010. 79.

and acceptable, and perfect, will of God."
Romans 12: 1-2

What God is saying when He speaks through Paul on this issue of transformation is a complete change – a spiritual change and a moral change. This is God's call on your life to make that change and completely surrender your soul to your Creator. When you do this, you are now on the threshold of becoming a disciple. Now, you must grow into the likeness of your Lord and Savior Jesus Christ which is a lifetime journey with God the Holy Spirit, and those that God has placed in your life.

Together, as a body of Christ, we all need to begin this journey. So, the $64,000 question is, how can we accomplish this task? One way is to allow your small group to develop into your small home church. When people are gathered together in a home church, they will grow in many ways that will bring glory to God and blessings to others. This doesn't mean you need to throw out the traditional church. Teach the people to gather throughout the week and worship God in a small home church through the small group on mission and then on Sunday, they will all come to the traditional church and gather and celebrate all that God is doing in, and through, them during the week. Let's be honest, drive by most churches on Monday and you will find a cold, closed building. Expand your mind and lose control and allow God to be glorified by doing God's Church – God's Way.

Priority Solution # 2 – Let me ask you this question – How did Jesus accomplish this task? How did Jesus teach others about love? How did Jesus transform the religious minds of the men around Him into the open and loving minds that desired to be like their Master?

Small Group Missional Format –

"And they, continuing daily with one accord in the temple, and breaking bread from house to house, did eat their meat with gladness and singleness of heart. Praising God and having favor with all the people. And the Lord added to the church daily such as should be saved." Acts 2: 46 – 47

The answer is found in the Small Group Missional Format. I know in America we love to grow everything as big as we can. I, like many of you, always thought that it would be so great if I was a leader of a mega church. The older I got in life and the more I learned about God, I realized that the answer wasn't found in bigger but amazingly, the answer is found in smaller. The name I choose for the small group format is what I call "Missional Communities." The main reason is that every small group formed must first be on mission with God. We must humbly accept God's invitation to join Him on mission. Also, the second word in that descriptive name is communities. A community is a gathering of people with a connectedness of a commonality that draws them closer to each other and to God. Each missional community will have a different mission assigned to them by God.

Benefit # 1: The first benefit of doing God's Church God's Way is extending love to God by serving God in accordance with His Word. We never see mega anything in the life of Christ or the early church. We see the gathering of small groups loving God and loving each other. It is said we are to love God with all our hearts, souls, and minds and I can't think of a better way to grow in this love and express this love to God than loving God in accordance with His Word.

Benefit # 2: When we serve God in the small missional community, we are serving each other. If we would do this, we would be in the act of making disciples. We would help grow each other through love and service. We would be teaching others how to grow closer to God by growing closer to each other. We would be on mission to include the making of disciples by inspiring and encouraging each other to grow and be more like Christ. This is what true discipleship is and means. This is not only a great way to learn and grow in Christ but to learn about and grow closer to others. We truly are missionaries that are striving together to teach each other and at the same time to learn from each other. There is a oneness element in this concept that man loves to reject but it is essential to the plan of God.

Benefit # 3: One answer to this complex problem is found in the word – *INTIMACY*! Jesus had a loving and intimate relationship with his apostles. One reason is that He loved them and there wasn't 1,000 of them but only twelve. Let us not split hairs, I know there were more people in His ministry than twelve and I acknowledge the truth that many women played key roles in His ministry. Since I don't know the total number, and though I don't believe that number was a huge number, I am safe to only focus on the twelve disciples/apostles of Jesus Christ. In this small missional community, you will find a deeper intimate relationship with others than you will ever find at the traditional church. As you grow in intimacy, you will want to share this concept with others at the church service on Sunday and this will draw others into joining your small group. Intimacy is a major factor in a relationship with God and with others. In this world today, we push away from intimacy because we really don't want others to know our real, true selves. However, this is part of the plan of God that draws us out and into the light. When we are in an intimate, trusting relationship, we are more open and honest which makes us very vulnerable. It is through this experience of being so vulnerable that we can find a peace and love unlike we have ever experienced before in our life. The deeper the intimacy, the deeper love we will grow into, and then begin to share it with others.

Benefit # 4: Loving others is a great benefit. When

we have the closeness of a missional community, we find safety and security to be ourselves. When we allow this closeness to draw us in deeper, we find the intimacy we need to grow in love. When we are close and intimate, we find that we can love and be loved by others, and that will give you an experience with God and others that you have never allowed yourself to possess in your life. Now you are love and can share love in the truest of forms.

I haven't shared this concept with you in this book but allow me to do this now. I believe after much research, studying, and praying that I am sure you, or your soul, was created in heaven. On day six in the Bible, Genesis 1: 26 -27 of the creation processes, God created man in His own image and likeness. Where did He do this? It was not until Genesis 2: 7 that God formed the physical man and breathed into him life. I believe that God breathed man's soul into his body and in that process, gave man life. So, I believe that God created all the souls of mankind in heaven and has allowed each soul to be united with the physical body over the entire history of time.

If this is true, your soul was created by God, who is love, and you are love and experienced existence in heaven, in love, until you came to earth by divine power. Once we entered sin, we needed our souls restored into the image of God and this only happens through the plan of salvation offered by Jesus Christ. Allow me to ask you this question – Other than elements like air, water, and food, and things like this, what is one element that you can think of that you share the need of, with all mankind? I say it is love. Isn't it interesting that all mankind for most of their lives are in search of this mysterious element that is called love? I believe that all mankind was created in love, experienced love, and shared love in heaven prior to being sent to earth. We continue to crave this love found in God and in other human beings. We are in search of the love of God, which is God, and to experience the love we knew in heaven with others here on earth. If I am correct, this is one of the reasons that the American Church is dying. We are trying to please others instead of connecting them to love. People have lost interest and value in the church because they are in search of love not comfort. This is also why the truth of the small missional community and the small home church community is so valuable like it was in the time of Jesus.

Lastly, if I am correct in my understanding of where our souls were created and our existence in and with God, it is amazing how we grow best in small missional communities. Jesus chose this format, and therefore it is the best template for us to return to for His glory and our blessings!

Traditional Churches

It is clear in the book of Acts that they met not only in the temple but also house to house daily as they utilized the small group format. Also, a better example could not be found for the Christ United Ministry in the development of disciples than that of the same format used by Jesus Christ and the Apostles.

It is based on this format that Jesus Christ and the early church operated and were successful in reaching the millions of new converts over the early years. We have chosen to no longer follow the template that Jesus and the early church successfully used, and we must return to this format if we seek to *DO GOD'S CHURCH IN GOD'S WAY!*

Here is a *MAJOR POINT* in this process that has generated so much hate, fear, and push back on me and my wife as we have offered this to the local churches. The leadership of the church must understand that God's way of doing His Church is extending love to a dying community. The main thing that needs to change is the heart of leadership. The change that needs to occur is found on Monday – Saturday through the mobilization and missional small group to penetrate the community. If leadership will make the commitment to God through the development of small missional groups, I will guarantee you that the congregation will accept, albeit slowly, but they will accept it. Most people we have spoken with over the years, only hear the truth that the American Church is dying and the reasons why. They have never stayed around long enough, due to their shallow way of thinking, to hear the truth.

If you are a leader/pastor of a local Church in America,

your Sunday worship service should continue to operate the way it has, though I would encourage you to make it more celebratory in nature and lift up the name of Jesus Christ and preach His gospel. However, other than that, and those are big, you operate the same, so you need not fear change.

It is the Monday – Saturday efforts that need to be encompassed into your plan. The development of a small missional community isn't complex, but it is much more intricate than you may understand today. If you decide you want to begin to serve God and do God's Church in God's Way, call me and I will come and help you set a plan in action.

Step # 1 – Gather your leadership together and pray! Let God the Holy Spirit lead you to be successful in this effort. God knows how He wants to run His body – *LET HIM*! Pray – Pray – Pray for God's divine intervention and presence throughout the entire process.

Step # 2 – Gather your congregation and softly and gently share with them the need to offer this to your community. All people hate and fear change so don't make this an overnight change. I am developing a workbook that will help you teach and inspire your congregation to participate in this effort. I would begin an open discussion of options and hopes for the future. Also, the Senior Pastor must be on-board with this effort because if he is not and he turns it over to another person, the congregation will smell this and reject this before it gets off the launching pad.

Step # 3 – The slow and gentle introduction of small missional communities into your church. Now, please don't try and rush this process just so you can be proud to have small groups. I have been excited to attend a church that is participating in the small missional group format, however, I have found leaders just change the name of their Sunday School classes to small groups! A total failure! This is not what you want to do as you will never be able to introduce true small missional groups in your church. This step is like the saying, "How do you eat an elephant? One spoonful at a time!" Go slow and take small steps. This is new to everyone and remember – people hate change. Help them adjust to the new idea and even help them make it their idea.

True small missional communities should consist of a total number of approximately 12 – 15 people. Here is a secret that many people miss. The small missional group should consist of about 4 or 5 dedicated Christian disciples that are committed to penetrating the community to reach the lost for Jesus Christ. If you have 4 or 5 Christians in your group, they each will invite one or two non-Christian people that they know to the group and that will bring your total up to 12 – 15 people.

You may ask why so small? Well, a small missional group offers a more intimate environment to all and that gives everyone a chance to get to know each other on a deeper level. Also, *THIS IS IMPORTANT* – the small missional community is formed out of a common interest of the leader(s). My wife Vicki began her missional group and called it "Feeding Angels Cooking Club!" The group is focused on getting together each week for an hour or two and one is the leader and makes a recipe and walks everyone through the preparations of this meal. Then, and this is a fun part, everyone gets to eat the meal together. People love it! Now, pay attention to this part, she has yet to offer a prayer over the meal or talk about God in this group. You may be shocked but watch how this unfolds. The 3 – 4 Christians in her group are busy developing a relationship with the people who don't know Jesus. They are developing an intimate and deep relationship as they meet each week and then even get together a few times for lunch or coffee just to talk and grow in their relationship. They like each other!

Now, how many times have you asked a friend or family member to come to your church? They look at you like a deer in the head lights and they don't want to lie but they don't want to come so they say, I will try to make it, and you know they won't. Well, when you hold a small missional community like this, you invite someone who has the same interest, they jump at the chance to learn and eat! You don't want to introduce prayer, bible study, or a discussion of Jesus until they are so comfortable in your relationship. Before you try to share the gospel with another person in today's world, you must build the

RELATIONSHIP. Once they accept you, they are more willing to accept the gospel.

Vicki even offers a separate night of the week where the group can get together and take the food to people that they know could use a good meal. Watch this – This is the mission that God has invited her into through the development of her group. They learn to cook and eat together but their mission is to take the food they prepare to those less fortunate and feed them. When a person that is not connected to Jesus sees, and experiences, the art of sharing love with others by feeding them, they are drawn closer to the group and are more open to wanting to know more. When the time is right, you can share the gospel. When you have developed a strong relationship built on love and trust that person is ready to follow you to trust Jesus. I call this *SHOWING THE LOVE OF JESUS, AND THEN AT THE RIGHT TIME, SHARING THE GOSPEL OF JESUS.* Once a person sees the love and then hears about the love, they are more willing to accept Jesus Christ as their Lord and Savior.

Now watch this – once they are a believer, you can ask them to join you at church and *NOW* they will want to follow you. I call this *LOVING THEM INTO HEAVEN AND THEY WILL FOLLOW YOU TO CHURCH.* It doesn't matter if you attend a traditional church or a home church – they will follow you to church. You will build your group and have a blast. You will be on mission with God to share love to the community. You will be showing and sharing the gospel of Jesus Christ and you will be loving others into heaven and into church! *BOOM!*

Allow me to make this point – the mission your group will take is not your decision. The leaders of a group will gather and pray over this until they know what God wants them to do as *HE INVITES US INTO HIS MISSION.* Don't make the mistake of calling a mission of God before you know what the mission of God is to be. Also, and this is *IMPORTANT,* you don't want to start a small missional community on campus or at the church. Let's be honest – people have no interest in going to your church at this point. Form your small missional community off campus, out of your home if possible. When you invite someone to your home, they are more willing to come than if you ask them to come to your church building. People will reject and push back simply because they have no interest, and see no value, in the church. If possible, form your small missional community off campus and at your home.

Again, this is Monday – Saturday activities that has nothing to do with the church. The traditional church should be excited to be a part of this as this is how God will grow His church! All you must do is slowly introduce small missional communities like Vicki's to your congregation and watch how excited people will be to join to serve God by serving each other. You will see groups take on a life of their own. You will see some groups grow rapidly and some slow. You will see some groups start a mid-week Bible Study after their missional group time because they want to grow in Christ together more and they all draw closer. Just don't push this until your group is ready.

Non-Traditional Churches or Non-Churched Groups

I believe deeply and desperately in my heart that most people desire to be connected to God. They just have no idea how to do this. The church has failed, leaving millions of people lost in the dark. There is an answer!

Home Churches -

Everything that you have read about small missional communities will be the same for the non-churched small group and the non-traditional churches. Vicki and I have a small home church and it will serve the small groups of people that are ready to share love and worship God together, but they don't want to attend a church building. Let's be honest, some people have been hurt very badly by the church. Many people have experienced such pain they will never walk into a church building again. Some people simply have never been in a church and have little or no interest in doing so. Love people where they are and meet their need by loving them right there!

The answer is forming a small home missional church that will consist of about 15 – 20 people. Just like your mid-week small group, you don't want it to grow too large as you will lose the intimacy with others. People want to be connected to God and to others. Don't take that away from them by trying to build a bigger home church. Your mid-week small missional community will be on mission for God. Those who become connected to God through Christ Jesus, will want to join you at your home missional church. Cole states, "Coming into a living room and finding a close-knit spiritual family where everyone is involved, each praying and singing and sharing his or her inner life, is quite amazing for someone who has not learned to trust yet. Sensing the power of Christ working in and through such people can break open any heart."[217] Don't be upset if a new convert decides they would like to join a bigger more traditional church. It is important to be gathered with other Christians for your growth so don't stand in their way.

One problem I have encountered with people who I have spoken with on this subject is that they don't feel qualified to teach if they were to start a home church. This is an important issue not to be taken lightly. I have read a lot of different opinions on this issue such as Neil Cole, who believes that it is best to just have lay persons run the home church. I disagree. I believe that God calls His pastors/shepherds to lead His church and a home church is probably the closest church to His call than

---

[217] Cole, Neil. *Church 3.0: upgrades for the future of the church*. San Francisco, CA: Jossey-Bass Publishing. 2010. 49.

all the rest. I believe a home missional church needs one qualified and called pastor to lead. This pastor/shepherd can lead many home churches through the utilization of the internet and developing a strong lay person leadership network under him. The biggest problem I have with not having a qualified and called man of God is, the church can suffer and then the church can be on a slippery slope. I am called as a shepherd and it is my job to protect the flock from wolves (Satan/Demons) and the church can suffer greatly if they leak into your church. Liberalism/secularism can creep into your home church just like it has the larger traditional churches and destroy your church so a strong leader that is qualified and called can lead in accordance to God's Word.

Lastly, a missional home church may not seem like an option today for some readers. However, allow me to remind you that one of the reasons the 1st Century Christians utilized home churches was due to persecution. As we have entered the end times one would be blind to not see how the persecution of Christians is on the rise – and *NOT* just in other countries. The United States of America will soon be taxing the traditional churches in a way to effectively close them. We are already seeing how the laws are being passed to control what is preached in the church. In Canada today, you can be arrested and jailed for preaching against homosexuality in the streets of Toronto. Persecution will again be a high price for Christians to pay if we are to hold to our faith. Don't forget that many home churches in China today, gather in crawl spaces of homes to worship God and to avoid persecution.

I recently had a friend of mine tell me that this idea of small missional communities and missional home churches that I share has made me years ahead of my time. I told him that I didn't agree due to the dying of the American Church and the need to begin to do God's Church – God's Way. However, don't be surprised when one day soon the landscape of our country is changed, and we will be under severe persecution. Just another reason to accept and adopt this new plan for the church.

Chapter 11

Congregational Integrity

"The integrity of the upright shall guide them:
but the perverseness of transgressors shall destroy them."
Proverbs 11: 3

Church Problem # 5:

I spoke on this earlier and said that I would confront the congregations of the dying churches later in this book – The Time Is Now! I must confront the congregations at this point. Many people will act shocked that this is even an issue for the church. You may be saying, "How can he blame us?" First, I'm not blaming anyone. I am pointing out that the dying of God's Church is a problem that is shared by all of us. It is all our sins that has caused Jesus to spew us out. So, don't let pride (sin) enter and move you to shut your mind or heart to the truth.

The main problem with the congregations of today is that we have developed a consumer attitude toward church. We feel that we must have the soft seats, the nice lighting, the best sound systems, the concert experience in the musical venue, the preaching that won't offend us but simply make us feel good, and a leadership team that is going to make sure we are happy and reject anything that could cause a problem that would make people choose to leave. People shop church today like they shop Walmart for food. I admit when I was single, I went to Walmart when I wasn't feeling good, to buy some soup. I was amazed at the rows upon rows of different cans of soup available. They had everything available to make me happy so that ultimately, I would buy at least one can of soup. I was so disheartened that I simply left the store because there were too many choices.

The church today tries to please everyone by accomplishing at least one thing for everyone thereby ensuring they are taking care of the consumer with a wide range of choices. Church, God's Church, was never intended to operate this way. The congregation was never supposed to develop this mentality toward church. You are supposed to go to church to *WORSHIP GOD. PERIOD!*

Many times, a congregation will take on the image of their leadership. This can be a huge problem for a church and one that can aid in the death process for a church. Do you remember the story that I spoke of earlier about the Baptist Church in need of a pastor? This church has a leadership issue, but the image transferred to the congregation. Watch how this works.

Once the lies and gossip from the leadership began to filter into the congregation, it was like a death warrant on us. I was so baffled as to the change in the friendliness to unfriendliness, the warmth to coldness, the love to dislike, the push out instead of the embrace inward. To this day I have no idea why these people changed. They are church people. Jesus said of religious people of His day, hypocrites, pretenders, liars, and fake people. When they thought we were just visitors to their church – they were excited probably to help them in donations and collections. When they found out who we were through gossip and lies, they rejected us. Don't get me wrong, if you meet me and discuss something with me and walk away and reject me as a person, I accept your decision. To reject someone that you have never spoken with or had a conversation with on a subject, but only listened to lies and gossip, you should be in jail. Lastly, no one from this church ever called on us to minister or pray with us and discuss why we were no longer attending their church. Good religious people!

Many church folks don't get it. Many think the world is lost and they own the keys to heaven. What they don't understand is that the behavior they display to the world is what killed their church. Many are pretentious with attitudes of the elites and this is one reason the community isn't coming to their church. All the people that live around a church, and have no interest in attending that church, should be all the information they need to know that the church is the problem. Allow me to illustrate my point. Let's say that a church sits in a neighborhood. There are approximately 1,000 homes in the vicinity which leads one to believe that there is approximately 4,000 people (1,000 homes x four people in a family) that live around the church. How many people attend a small neighborhood church? Let's estimate that about 100 people attend this church. 3,900 people find no value in your church or in you as a Christian! The problem is that the 100 people go to church – run inside the church building – and praise Jesus that they are saved, and they say they feel bad for those outside the church. Hooey! The people of a church like this are the reason that people outside are not connected to God and, believe me, they will pay for their actions. They just don't seem to understand that they are the problem. Here is a truth you can write down: "The world is rejecting God because they are rejecting the people who say they are of God." I cannot tell you how many times I have heard this phrase: "If that man is a Christian, I don't want any part of being a Christian." That is a sad indictment on the church. A reminder of what Macchia states is, "The goal of a healthy church is to raise the standards for the congregation in effectively loving God through Christ-honoring generosity."[218] The people of your community don't know God, but they know you and they *REJECT* you, so they reject God. The

---

[218] Macchia, Stephen A. *Becoming a Healthy Church: 10 Traits of a Vital Ministry.* Grand Rapids, MI: Baker Books. 1999. 212.

community is rejecting your church. There are thousands of people around your church, but you only have 100 people who attend your church. Do you think that *YOU MAY BE THE PROBLEM*?

The leadership of the church infects the congregation and vice-versus and you have a deadly combination. Many congregations of many churches have fallen prey to laziness, apathy, and consumerism and they expect the leadership to cater to these attitudes and in many ways, entertain them. If this is your church, please show me in the Bible where God says this is how He designed His church?

IS YOUR CHURCH SUFFERING FROM CONGREGATIONAL INTEGRITY? YES NO
If yes, your church needs reformation and change. Read On!

Reformation # 5:

The congregations of our churches today are as responsible for the action of Jesus spewing us out as anything else in the church. We must stop for a moment and re-think our decisions in attending church today. Do you attend a church for any reason other than to worship God? Let me be honest, most leadership boards of churches struggle with this issue. How do you hire a true called man of God who will bring the truth of God, moving the Holy Spirit over the congregation convicting them of sin, and sharing the gospel of Jesus Christ to a group of people who are only there for social reasons? How does a pastor keep his job and bring the truth to a people that are only there once a week to connect with friends and family? How does a leadership board of a church develop an evangelic outreach plan that is designed to penetrate the community and reach the lost when the people only look to the pastor to "get people saved?"

If you attend a "family" church which is a small church that consists of one or two families and you are not growing as you are exclusive and rejecting of anyone that is not of your family or close friends, what will be your answer be to God, who says, "did you love me or yourself?" If you attend a mega church because you like the concert each week and you can play on your phone during the messages, what will you say when God says, "did you love others?" If you attend a church that is dying because you never stood up to the leadership and accepted the commandments of making disciples, what will you say when God says, "did you make disciples?" You will be called before God to give an account of your life, which includes your life with God and others. What will be your answer?

The congregations of our churches must be the ones to stand up and admit that their church is dying. They must then call the leadership board and the pastor and hold them accountable for not standing up to, and for you. Then, and only then, you, as the body of Christ, must kneel together confessing your sins to each other and to God, repenting of your sins by turning away from the sins and turning to God for guidance, and then seek forgiveness together. Once your congregation takes the responsibility and takes charge, then your church, the body of Christ, can begin to be obedient to God's Word and adhere to the commandments of God and love others by making disciples.

The question now becomes how does the congregation begin to obey the commandments of God? In this book, we have discussed the need for small missional groups and how they can have an impact on a community. The congregations must stand up to the leadership and *DEMAND* that the leadership put this concept of missional groups into their church. The best way to accomplish this task is first to hold meetings with leadership and pastor(s) to ascertain if you have enough information to begin this process. If not, then assign the pastor the responsibility, because he should have known of this, and allow him to formulate a plan to present to the congregation at a later date.

The congregation *MUST* hold the pastor accountable to complete this task in a reasonable amount of time. Once he presents a few different options to the congregation on the best possible way to create and develop these missional groups, then the congregation and leadership selects the ones best for them. You then implement these plans and in a matter of weeks, or a few months, the Body of

Christ will be formed into small groups of Christians on mission for, and with, God to penetrate the community and extend love to those who are disconnected from God. It isn't this simple, but with the right help and the right attitude, you can do this with the leadership of God the Holy Spirit.

This is the only solution to this problem. If we are to bring glory to God and blessings to each other, we must take responsibility and become accountable for our actions. Stop using God's House for your playground and get serious about going to church, being the church and worshiping God.

This is a very important point on this issue. I hope someone in your life taught you this lesson. You are the church of God. You are His representative in this world. As the church, you should be serving God everyday of the week and celebrating on Sunday with each other. Inspiring and encouraging each other as you prepare for another week of battling Satan and his vessels to continue to expand the kingdom of God on earth. This is a truth that you need to put in your heart and make your stand today before it is to late. Be the man or woman of God that He has blessed you to be and be the Light to the dying world that He demands you be!

Chapter 12

Denominational Lies

"There is one body, and one Spirit, even as ye
are called in one hope of your calling;
One Lord, one faith, one baptism, One God
and Father of all, who is above all,
and through all, and in you all."
Ephesians 4: 4 – 6

Church Problem # 6:

If you haven't noticed by now, in everything man touches - he makes a huge mess. We live in a broken and fallen world. Man has always tried to intervene and make decisions that he thought were better than the last guy's decisions because he had the best way. You can find this in the subject of denominational issues. Man can't get along on anything. Here is a powerful statement: There are no denominations in the Bible. Man, invented denominations to separate and divide mankind theologically. Denominations are the most divisive and destructive structures mankind has ever formed in his existence. The Bible is clear that man should only exalt the name of Jesus Christ and we all will fall on our knees before Him one day. If that day was today, we would be falling before Him as hypocrites. The following is a scripture that best fits this problem:

"Who changed the truth of God into a lie and worshipped and served the creature more than the Creator, who is blessed forever. Amen." Romans 1: 25

Is this not a truth? Everywhere you look, we see man changing what God has designed so that it best fits his desires. We truly have made the decision to worship the creation instead of the Creator. Now is the time for this to stop or we will not simply be in a death spiral, we will experience a much-deserved death.

Here is an example of our brokenness in relationship to simply exalting the name of Jesus. On Resurrection Sunday, as Christians, we cherish and celebrate the truth that Jesus was resurrected, and this gives us our hope. Other religions such as the Jewish Faith or the Muslims state that this event never happened. So, the focus is only on Christianity. However, when we take this example a step further, we see that Christian man has fought with Christian man over who resurrected Jesus. Watch this:

The Bible states this event in many places and in many ways; Jesus will resurrect Himself from the tomb (John 2: 19), The power of the Holy Spirit will raise Him up (Romans 8: 11), and God resurrected Jesus (1 Corinthians 6: 14). Man enters into the need to prove his doctrinal position on this event and if you disagree with him, then you are wrong, and he gains superiority over you. The simple fact is the God Head resurrected Jesus Christ from the tomb and He now sits at the right hand of the Father! *BOOM*! To argue this point only serves to bring Jesus Christ down to our level and we *ARE NOT EXALTING HIM*! The simple truth is that however a person understands this event, it will not determine their eternal salvation other than if they don't accept the truth that Jesus *WAS RESURRECTED*. So why do we spend so much time on arguing our points of how others must believe how we believe? This does not exalt Jesus Christ!

Another example of this is on the doctrine of soul sleep or the immediacy into the presence of Jesus Christ upon death. I witnessed my father and my uncle argue, and almost fight, on this issue. My father, a Baptist, and my uncle, a Seventh Day Adventist, disagreed on this doctrine and would get red faced and nose-to-nose in their disagreement. First, if you believe that you die and go immediately to Christ or if your soul sleeps until the resurrection, do either of these beliefs determine your eternal place? *NO*! As I watched man argue over this point, I did not feel that Jesus was *EXALTED*! Man was exalting his beliefs, power, and control over another! Is this what the Bible teaches? *NO!*

These two examples are how man is divided over a teaching of the Bible that has no effect on the eternal destiny of your soul. It does, however, bring the name of Jesus Christ down to man's level and that is exactly opposite to the teaching of Jesus Christ!

I want you to think about the overall attitude of your church as it relates to the issue of denomination. Let's say you are a Southern Baptist Denominational Church and someone that isn't connected to your denomination comes to your church – how is that person(s) treated? Do you simply love them and accept them, or do you begin your systematic judgement of that person? Allow me to illustrate this point.

We attended an Independent Baptist church in Arkansas not far from our home, and we were witnesses to this very fact. Vicki wanted to become more active in church so she asked if she could join the choir. The leadership said that would be a good thing and then began to give her a list of what she is to wear if she was going to be accepted into the choir. She was informed that if she didn't wear a skirt that was below the knees, she would not be allowed to join the choir.

How many stories have you heard about people being rejected from a church because they just didn't fit in with the others? The church is to love everyone and not sit in judgement of anyone. Many denominations are built on the theory that they are the "right" church and any that doesn't become a member of that denomination, they were simply lost. I will give you two major denominations that have shared that philosophy. The first one is the Church of Christ. At one time in history, though they have softened their stance on this issue today, they proclaimed that people need to be a member of the Church of Christ because they were the only people that would go to heaven. The second denomination is called the Landmark Baptist denomination. Again, like the Church of Christ today, they have soften their message but in their split from their main Baptist denomination, they offered to everyone that they had to belong to their denomination as they were the only ones that were going to heaven; everyone else was lost and going to hell. Where is that truth in the Bible? How many people did those statements and rejection by judgement hurt and drive away from Christ? Are we more desirous of people attending our church or of loving them into heaven?

IS YOUR CHURCH A RELIGIOUS DENOMINATION? YES NO
If yes, your church needs reformation and change. Read On!

Reformation Solution # 6:

I know this sounds like utopia, but isn't it time we stand united instead of being divided? Jesus says this:

"And Jesus knew their thoughts, and said unto them, every kingdom divided against itself is brought to desolation; and every city or house divided against itself shall not stand." Matthew 12: 25

This simple statement by Jesus is so appropriate to this subject and our time in history. If we continue to choose division through denominationalism, we will not only be divided and crumble, we will die. We must choose a different path – The Word of God is the path we must return to and reject the concept of man's path.

This may be the greatest hurdle for mankind to jump today because we live in a world of turmoil and tribulations where divisiveness is the flavor of the month, but we must stand by the truth and allow God to intervene and guide us back to His path. We must unite under the banner of "Jesus Christ" and be the people God has called and be the people of honor for the sake of all that Jesus Christ has done. Let us stand up as one, One Body – One Spirit – One Baptism and be the true people of God.

Chapter 13

Counting the Heads

"Not forsaking the assembling of our selves together,
as the manner of some is; but exhorting one another:
and so much the more, as ye see the day approaching."
Hebrews 10: 25

Church Problem # 7:

It seems everyone today is concerned with numbers. In the business world, it is the heartbeat of the organization. If you sell cars for a living and you know you must sell five cars a day to pay all the bills and put a few bucks in the bank, your focus will be on the number five. Again, if you run your church like an organization, you will be very concerned with counting the heads on Sunday mornings! I remember attending a Baptist church a long time ago and they would make it like a sales convention. The preacher would raise his voice and call out to the congregation and ask, "How many did you get saved this week?" People would yell back, "5" or "2" and I always yelled back "0." That caused the leadership to pause and I was asked why I didn't get anyone saved and I would remind them that I can't save anyone, and salvation is personal between God and man. They hated me!

The American Church is highly focused on how many people attend their church. They have lost their focus on the people; the people have become just a number. I know of a local church that runs a bus ministry and they pick up children for Sunday morning church only. They feed them breakfast and they have children's church and play games. They have little, if any, follow-up to reach the parents of these kids but are only concerned as to how many kids can they bring in the church. They count the heads of the kids as a number in attendance for their Sunday service. They are that desperate for numbers, so they say, "we had 170 in church Sunday," and they all applaud. However, 50 - 70 of that number were kids that really come to play and eat, and they have no other contact with them for the entire week!

As illustrated in the opening chapters, several people attending church, are people who have attended church for years. The church is declining in numbers as they are experiencing very little increase in numbers due to conversion of souls to Christ. The only small growth found in church today is transfer growth and that is when a person(s) transfer from another church to theirs and change their membership.

Let me ask you this question; Is your church having 5 – 10 people being reborn each week and walking the aisle to profess their faith in Christ. Is your church performing 5 – 10 baptisms each week helping others to identify with their new rebirth and proclaiming to the world their new love. Is your church growing in numbers with people who are attending or seeking membership into your church?

Let me not miss this important point. Just because a church has a lot of people in attendance, doesn't mean that it is a healthy church. They probably offer a great concert each week with great lighting and sound, or they are a popular church with a very popular preacher (and don't be misled, many popular preachers are false preachers in America). The point is, just because you attend a church along with a lot of other people, doesn't mean your numbers are healthy.

Most Churches in America, as demonstrated in previous chapters, are in decline or flat-lined in numbers. Even mega churches, if their numbers are not increasing, they may be flat-lined or even in decline so don't be fooled by a large number. Just as I will say, don't be fooled by a small number. The best churches in the world are small, but are very focused on serving God from a Biblical posture. However, the congregation is getting older and the younger generations find no value in the church, so they don't attend. If your church is not growing in conversion numbers, then you are probably a dying or dead church no matter the size of the church.

IS YOUR CHURCH FLAT-LINED OR IN DECLINE NUMBERICALLY? YES NO

If yes, your church is suffering and needs reformation and change. Read On!

Reformation Solution # 7:

The reformation that is needed in a church that is flat-lined or in decline is very simple. The entire church, congregation, leadership, and pastoral must first come together and confess the sin to each other and to God of apathy and lack of desire to serve God. This was the problem in the church of Laodicea, and this is the problem in the Church of America.

Together, this church must then work to obey the Bible and begin to love others by making disciples. The leadership must work closely with the pastor and congregation to raise the money to begin to penetrate the community. The pastor must begin to obey by raising up his flock to mature and grow in spiritual disciplines to have a stronger connection to God. The congregation must be willing to serve God by serving others and in unity, make the commitment to God to love others. All of this starts in church and doesn't leave until the power of the Holy Spirit covers and blesses them to grow. You must grow into a disciple before you can go out and make disciples.

Once this church has shared love together and grown in Christ, then they must GO into the world and begin to make disciples. Don't worry about getting people into your church, work to get them into heaven. If they are connected to God through your work, they will follow you to church. We don't need to focus on numbers when we are focused on the work. Focus on serving God and the numbers will take care of themselves.

The church must develop an evangelical outreach that is based in the small group format and this group must be on mission with God. When you do this, you will build a safe and intimate place for those not connected to God to find refuge. They will find security and safety in this missional group and this will open them up to a more intimate and loving relationship with you and ultimately with God.

This takes effort and commitment from your church. There is a saying in church that 90 percent of the work is done by 10 percent of the people and that is probably an accurate statement. Those days are gone! We need a 100 percent participation and commitment from the church to serve God by serving others. This is His commandment and we must be obedient to God! Our disobedience is the reason for our mess, let our obedience be the path to peace with God!

These few areas are the reformation that the church needs to begin to bring God's blessings to you and for you to bring glory to God. There are other areas of concern that we need to address but I think that if we can move in this direction that is contained in this book, we will be blessed by God, we will bring glory to God, and we will stand united and exalt the name of Jesus Christ. Let today be the day for the reformation of the Church of America to begin and let us continually look up for His grace to pour down on us as His people. Let us not be hypocrites and pretenders but be honest with ourselves and honest before God. We have failed and we confess our sins, we repent of our sins, and we seek forgiveness from the only One that can offer it. We then move in obedience to the Word of God to love God with all our hearts, souls, and minds - we love ourselves as our neighbors (Matthew 22: 37 – 39), and we love others showing the world that we truly are His disciples (John 13: 34 – 35).

Before we leave this chapter – How did you do on scoring your church? If you answered yes to 1- 3, your church is probably gasping for air and in a death spiral. If you answered yes to 4 – 5 questions, your church is in a comatose state and close to death. If you answered 6 -7 questions yes, your church is suffering and is dying and/ or moments from being dead. Be honest with yourself and others and draw close to God and confess and repent of your sins! If you find this is true about your church and are at the point of throwing up your hands in frustration, please reach out to me and I will be happy to come to your church and help you and your leadership team get on the path to peace and prosperity with God. There is *HOPE*! God doesn't want you to die, He wants you to do His Church – His Way!

Chapter 14

Revival for A Dying Church

"...to revive the spirit of the humble, and to
revive the heart of the contrite ones."
Isaiah 57: 15

Seven Biblical Principles for
Revival of a Dying Church

In this chapter, it is my desire is to connect the readers to
the Biblical principles of God that will bring revival to a
dying Church in America. As it has been communicated,
the need of the church to make disciples is of the upmost
importance. Putman states, "Discipleship is so much
more than just sharing the news about Jesus; it is also
about teaching people to obey the commands Jesus gave
us. Unfortunately, many churches have not taken this
charge seriously, and they are experiencing significant
problems."[219] Clearly, the Church of America is, and has

---

[219] Putman, *Real-Life Discipleship*, 21.

been, in sin for a long time and she must repent of this sin to avoid imminent death. One of the most prayed prayers of many is found in 2 Chronicles 7:14 but for some reason, it hasn't worked. America is still in trouble, her church is still in trouble, people are lost and in trouble, and many still pray this prayer. This author must confess that he also prayed this prayer for the church for years to no avail until God revealed a truth to him. Praying this prayer is only part of man's responsibility and this is where it gets hard to swallow. God promises to heal this land if man will do the following steps: humble, seek, pray, and turn from their wicked ways.

Life of the American Church lies in the first four Biblical principles of 2 Chronicles 7:14. It is imperative to realize that God opens this Scripture with the propositional word "If." God, knowing man, is saying *if* man will do this, He will do that in return. There is no guarantee that man will respond to God in the way that will move God to accomplish His part. When God spoke through the Chronicler, saying "If my people, who are called by my name," He was saying that Israel belonged to God as she was a nation with His name on her. Isaiah speaks to this issue as he says that others were never called by His name but only Israel was called like this.[220] Also, Jeremiah speaks to the same issue as he states, "we are your people,"[221] and seeks God to not leave them. Christians are His people

---

[220] Isaiah 63:19.
[221] Jeremiah 14:9.

who have been saved by the blood of Jesus Christ, His Son, and this is the mark of ownership of God on them. God is also speaking to the Christians in America as, "my people who are called by my name," as they read the Scripture found in 2 Chronicles. The Church of America needs to cry out to God as Jeremiah did begging God not to leave them, for they need His blessings. Falwell states, "Therefore, His requirement for national blessing was their seeking His face in true repentance (turn from their wicked ways). Only then could He remove their guilt and restore them to usefulness."[222] The Church of America needs His blessing to restore her so that she can become useful to God again.

Humility

In the understanding that God is speaking to His people, the first challenge to man is "to humble themselves." In the book of Micah, it says, "To do justly, to love mercy, and to walk humbly with your God."[223] This Scripture illustrates that God demands man to be totally devoted to Him and humbleness is an important issue of that devotion. Humility is the first Biblical principle for a revival for the Church of America. Vine's Dictionary defines the word humble as "lowliness of mind."[224] It

---

[222] Falwell, *Liberty Bible Commentary*, 810.

[223] Micah 6:8.

[224] Vine, Unger, and White Jr., *Vine's Complete Expository Dictionary of Old and New Testament Words, 314.*

is important for man to understand that he is not to be proud in the eyes of God. It is used always in a good sense in the NT, metaphorically, to denote a "of low degree, brought low...."[225] So man should also not be proud and haughty but also understand of how he is to be brought low before God, which is a good thing. Luke makes a statement of how those of low degree are exalted[226] and Paul refers to the same as he says, "but condescend to men of low estate."[227] God is the Great I Am and this alone should bring man to his knees in humbleness, a low position, before God.

Man does make a conscious choice of allowing his heart to become humble for God. John Dickson makes a powerful statement on the issue of humility, which is the act of being humble as he explains, "Humility is the noble choice to forgo your status, deploy your resources or use your influence for the good of others before yourself. More simply, you could say the humble person is marked by a willingness to hold power in service of others."[228] Humility is a choice. Man can stand in his own pride and power and attempt to continue to do what he believes is a good thing or he can choose to become humble at the feet of Jesus to understand His will. Once at the feet of Jesus, the overwhelming truth of who man is and what

---

[225] Ibid. 314.

[226] Luke 1:52.

[227] Romans 12:16.

[228] John Dickson, *Humilitas: A Lost Key to Life, Love, and Leadership* (Grand Rapids, MI: Zondervan, 2011), 24.

he has done is shown in the light of God – this leads man to the love of God. Benner expresses this as he says, "The humbling encounter with the depths of my sin leads to a love for God that is grounded in an appreciation for grace. And any genuine encounter with grace has the effect of deepening my love of others."[229] It is by God's grace that man can understand his failures and take the strength of God to stand up and continue his journey.

Prayer

Prayer is God's way for man to be connected to Him and for God to be connected to man. S. D. Gordon states, "In its simplest analysis prayer – all prayer – has, must have, two parts. First, a God to give…. just as certainly, there must be a second factor, a man to receive. Man's willingness is God's channel to the earth."[230] Many people in the world ask themselves, "What is the reason I'm here?" Some would want you to believe that this is a very complex and deep question, however, this author says that the answer is simple. Man was created to be in union with God. God desires man to enter into a deep, loving relationship with Himself found in the union with God. In possibly the most well-known of all Scriptures is John 3:16, "For God so loved the world, that he gave his only begotten Son that whosoever believeth in him should not perish but have everlasting life." God created man

---

229 Benner, *Surrender to Love*, 99.
230 S. D. Gordon, *Quiet Talks on Prayer* (Grand Rapids, MI: Mercy Place, 2003), 10.

in His image[231] and man lost this image in the Garden of Eden due to sin.[232] Since this time, man has needed a Savior for the forgiveness of his sins and to be restored to the union with God which can only happen through the salvation process. God, knowing this great need of man, sent His Son Jesus to this world to be man's Redeemer.[233] Jesus Christ says no man can return to the Father but by Him.[234] Man must be reborn into the family of God and this is by faith in the blood of Jesus Christ for the forgiveness of sins and the resurrection by the power of the Holy Spirit.

The journey is found in Jesus Christ who is the "Way" back to the Father and eternal life in heaven. Benner states, "The image of journeying with Jesus highlights the relational nature of Christian spirituality…. They are invited to follow Jesus – that is, travel with Jesus."[235] In this journey, one finds that the perfect love of Jesus Christ is the example for their life on earth. Daniel Lancaster states, "Prayer introduces learners to Jesus as the Holy One. He lived a holy life and died for us on the cross. God commands us to be saints as we follow Jesus."[236] As man's example, Jesus taught His disciples, as well as all Christians, to pray. One of the most powerful

---

[231] Genesis 1:26.

[232] Genesis 3:6.

[233] John 6:38.

[234] John 14:6.

[235] Benner, *Surrender to Love, 107.*

[236] Daniel B. Lancaster, *Making Radical Disciple* (Gardena, CA: T4T Press, 2011), 73.

Scriptures on this subject is found in Matthew 6:9–13, "After this manner therefore pray ye: Our Father which art in heaven, Hallowed be thy name. Thy Kingdom come. Thy will be done in earth, as it is in heaven. Give us this day our daily bread. And forgive us our debts, as we forgive our debtors. And lead us not into temptation but deliver us from evil: For thine is the kingdom, and the power, and the glory, forever. Amen." The blueprint for connecting with the Father is found in the teachings of Jesus on prayer. Clearly, the church is not in obedience to God and not making disciples, an important part of this prayer is the need for forgiveness of our "debts" which are our sins. Elmer Towns says, "When you pray "Forgive us our debts," you are praying as a child of the Father who has not lived up to your Father's expectation. You are saying "I'm sorry" to your heavenly Father so you can have fellowship with Him again."[237]

Sin weakens fellowship with God and causes a breach in the relationship and it is necessary for man to pray for the forgiveness of sin for that relationship to be restored. Some sins of man that have caused this disobedience to God are very strong sins that need powerful prayer. Elmer Towns addresses the issue of besetting sins that have plagued man to disobey God as he says, "Besetting sins are habitual sinful behaviors or attitudes that victimize

---

[237] Elmer L. Towns, *Praying the Lord's Prayer for Spiritual Breakthrough: Daily Praying The Lord's Prayer As A Pathway Into His Presence* (Ventura, CA: Regal Books, 1997), 145.

and enslave people…. Any sin that can't be broken with ordinary "willpower" can be termed a besetting sin."[238]

Prayer of man is the only way to be connected to God as man lives in the kingdom of Satan and yet to return to heaven. Jesus taught to pray that God's Kingdom Come and His will be done which is calling on God in prayer for His Kingdom to reign here on earth. Gordon says, "Prayer is man giving God a footing on the contested territory of this earth. The man in full touch of purpose with God praying, insistently praying – that man is God's footing on the enemy's soil…. And the Holy Spirit within that man, on the new spot, will insist on the enemy's retreat in Jesus the Victor's name. That is prayer."[239] When one couples this statement with the Scripture found in the book of James 4:7 as he says, "Submit yourselves therefore to God. Resist the devil, and he will flee from you," clearly there is power in prayer. Dave Earley says, "Spiritual work depends upon spiritual tools. No spiritual tool is as significant or powerful as prayer."[240]

Prayer is a spiritual tool that possesses great power. Spurgeon states, "If we are truly humble-minded we shall not venture down to the fight until the Lord of Hosts has clothed us with all power, and said to us, "Go in this thy

---

[238] Elmer L. Towns, *Fasting for Spiritual Break Through: A Guide To Nine Biblical Fasts* (Ventura, CA: Regal Books, 1996), 30.

[239] Gordon, *Quiet Talks on Prayer,* 26.

[240] Dave Earley, *Prayer: The Timeless Secret of High-Impact Leaders* (Chattanooga, TN: Living Ink Books, 2008), 2.

might."[241] The words, "clothed us with all power," is an inspiring passage that moves the heart to know that God's will can be done but only after one has prayed.

God's desire is that His will be done so He does expect man to pray so that He can sustain man in his journey in this life. Paul taught in the book of Colossians that man is to be devoted to prayer[242] and also found in the book of 1 Thessalonians; Paul teaches that Christians should be continually praying.[243] Whitney states, "God expects every Christian to be devoted to prayer and to pray without ceasing."[244] It is clear that God expects man to pray and that there is power in prayer for man to find forgiveness and move God to restore man to righteousness but man must be devoted to God to pray in this manner.

Seeking God

Man must seek God, which deepens the relationship between God and man. The relationship is deepened as man seeks and is guided by God into His truth. Due to the nature of man, God knew he would need assistance to find the power to seek God, so He provides this help in the person of the Holy Spirit. John Walvoord states, "In addition to natural inability is the work of Satan blinding the hearts of the lost to the light of the gospel

---

[241] Spurgeon, *Lectures to My Students,* 48.
[242] Colossians 4:2.
[243] 1 Thessalonians 5:17.
[244] Whitney, *Spiritual Disciplines for The Christian L.I.F.E,* 68.

(2 Cor.4:4). The condition of man is hopeless apart from divine intervention."[245] This is evidenced in Scriptures as God draws man to Himself, for man would not seek God without God's power to aid him. Jesus speaks to this issue as He states in John 6:44, "No man can come to me, except the Father which hath sent me draw him: and I will raise him up at the last day." Man, in his natural state does not possess the desire for the understanding of God's truth. John Walvoord adds, "Man in himself is utterly unable to understand the truth of God. The answer to the problem, therefore, is not found in any development of the natural man or cultivation of latent abilities, but is disclosed in the power of God as manifested in the work of the Holy Spirit."[246] God moves on whomever He chooses but without God's power, it is clear that man couldn't seek Him. Charles Ryrie states, "The Spirit's work is sovereign; he touches whom He wills to touch, just as the wind blows where it pleases (John 3:8). He works according to the sovereign purposes of God in His elective grace."[247] God the Holy Spirit is submissive to the Father and moves in accordance to His will and man can only see the effects of the Holy Spirit much like the effects of the wind. According to Carson, "The point is that wind can be neither controlled nor understood by human

---

[245] John F. Walvoord, *The Holy Spirit.* 3rd ed (Grand Rapids, MI: Zondervan, 1966), 110.

[246] Ibid. 110.

[247] Charles C. Ryrie, *The Holy Spirit. Revised and Expanded* (Chicago, IL: Moody Publishers, 1997), 35.

beings…. But that does not mean we cannot detect the wind's effects. Where the Spirit works, the effects are undeniable and unmistakable."[248] God, knowing man's nature, aids him through the power of the Holy Spirit to seek God to draw closer and to grow in his relationship with God.

Jesus spoke to His disciples on the issue of seeking as He said in Matthew 6:33, "But seek ye first the kingdom of God, and his righteousness; and all these things shall be added unto you." Jesus chose the Greek word *zeteo* which means, according to Vine, "to seek or strive after, endeavor, to desire."[249] The Greek word also denotes that this seeking be a continual or constant seeking. Man, empowered by the Holy Spirit, is always motivated and encouraged to be in the process of seeking God with the desire to find the truth of God. Man must be seeking God with a desire to return to Him in obedience so that the church can again become effective servants of His to make disciples.

Confession

The Bible clearly states the truth as it says, "If we confess our sins, he is faithful and just to forgive us our sins, and to cleanse us from all unrighteousness."[250] When

---

[248] Carson, *The Gospel According to John*, 197.

[249] Vine, Unger, and White, Jr, *Vine's Complete Expository Dictionary of Old and New Testament Words*, 558.

[250] 1 John 1: 9

we come in humbleness before the Throne of God with a heart that is willing to confess our sins, God is faithful! We are mere men and we are broken and flawed. Each time in our lives we must come to the truth on an issue and many times this should lead us to His Throne in humbleness to confess we sinned against Him. It is when we try and hide from God and deny we are sinners is when we get into real trouble. It is God's mercy we need as taught in the Bible, "Whoever conceals their sins does not prosper, but the one who confesses and renounces them finds mercy." It is in His mercy that we can confess and become prosperous and doesn't the church need exactly that today?

Also, a point needs to be made that we not only need to confess to God our sins, but we need to seek each other and confess our sins to them. I speak of the church – the pastors/leaders and the congregations! If our churches have been spat out by Jesus due to our sins, we must not only confess to God but confess to each other as stated, "Therefore confess your sins to each other and pray for each other so that you may be healed. The prayer of a righteous person is powerful and effective."[251] Did you catch that one word – healed? The American Church needs to be HEALED! Only God can heal us, and he will heal us when we take the steps, He has lined out in His word for a people who have sinned against Him.

---

[251] James 5: 16 (NIV)

Repentance

Man is repeatedly informed in the Bible of the need to repent. God loves His children, but he will discipline them for disobedience as seen in the book of Revelation 3:19, "As many as I love, I rebuke and chasten: be zealous therefore, and repent." In the New Testament, there is a need for man to repent from the disbelief of the fact that Jesus Christ is the Messiah which brings about salvation of one's soul. Jesus clearly teaches the need for man to repent as He states in Matthew 4:17, "Repent: for the kingdom of heaven is at hand." Repentance, according to Walter Elwell, "meaning to turn back, away from, or toward"[252] gives one a clear understanding that man must turn back or away from their old belief system and turn toward God to receive His truth that Jesus is the Messiah. Allen Myers adds, "Repentance may represent only regret or remorse over a past thought or action…. but in its fullest sense it is a term for a complete change of orientation involving a judgment upon the past and a deliberate redirection for the future….As such it is the subjective human experience involved in conversion."[253] Repentance is necessary for man to change his complete orientation of his life and turn away from sin and turn to God for forgiveness.

---

[252] Elwell, *Evangelical Dictionary of Theology,* 1012.
[253] Allen C. Myers, ed, *The Eerdmans Bible Dictionary* (Grand Rapids, MI: William B. Eerdmans Publishing Company, 1987), 880.

Though the aforementioned information is offered on a personal basis for man, the Bible is clear that as a people of God, there is also a need for repentance. In the Scripture used for the premise of this section of the project, 2 Chronicles found in the Old Testament, Solomon is dedicating the temple to God. God makes promises to Solomon and mankind to be their God in good times and bad times – in times of obedience and in times of disobedience. According to Lawrence Richards, "Calling on God as a covenant-keeping Person, Solomon rehearsed some of the promises God had given His people, speaking both of God's commitment to discipline Israel when she sinned and to forgive and restore when Israel returned to the Lord."[254] God is clearly in the business of promising to love His people, personally and corporately. John Walvoord and Roy Zuck offer their insight on this issue as they state, "God then encouraged Solomon by the promise that if His judgment (by drought, locusts, or a plague) should fall on the nation for their sin, they need only turn to the Lord in earnest humility and repentance and they would find forgiveness and restoration."[255] God is saying that they need only to turn to the Lord in repentance to find forgiveness and this must be the nderstanding for the Church of America. Another

---

[254] Lawrence O. Richards, *The Teacher's Commentary: Explains and Applies the Scriptures in A Way That Will Help You Teach Any Lesson from Genesis To Revelation* (Colorado Springs, CO: Scripture Press Publications, 1987), 249.

[255] John F. Walvoord and Roy Zuck, *The Bible Knowledge Commentary: An Exposition of the Scriptures by Dallas Seminary Faculty* (Wheaton, IL: Victor Books, 1983), 626.

example of a time when the people of God needed to repent, seek forgiveness of sins, and return to God can be found in the book of Nehemiah.[256] Nehemiah seeks God's mercy and forgiveness for not only his sins, but the sins of his fathers, as well as the children of Israel. Clearly, when a person or a nation turns back to God in obedience to His commandments, He is merciful to forgive and restore them by His grace. Corporately, the Church of America has great need to repent and turn back to God, away from her sins of apathy and apostasy, and return to obedience for His glory and for the church's blessings. God is expressly stating that man and the church have a great need for repentance as He says, "and turn from your wicked ways."[257]

Forgiveness

If you have ever read the Bible cover to cover, you know that man is inherently flawed and broken and in great need of forgiveness. In our society, and in our churches, we don't like to discuss the truth that we sin. Sin is not a word we like to discuss anywhere, and the reason is that if we understand that we sin, we must be moved to ask for forgiveness. Let me ask all the married people reading this book, is there a day that goes by you don't feel the need to be forgiven by your wife for something, small or big, that you did or said that hurt her? Allow me to ask you also,

---

[256] Nehemiah 1:1–11.
[257] 2 Chronicles 7:14.

is there a day that goes by that you didn't do something, small or big, that you hurt God? We are human and we make many mistakes and are sinful people. I thank God for my salvation found in the forgiveness by Jesus Christ and I wish I didn't sin but every day I do sin. I am not perfect, I am saved! God through Paul is talking to all of man, saved and unsaved, as he states, "For all have sinned, and come short of the glory of God."[258] Everyday we need to seek God for forgiveness of our sins.

When we come in humbleness and confess our sins, our hearts are opened to move us to ask God to forgive us of our sins we have committed. Is the American Church in need of asking and being forgiven of our sins?

Obedience

Jesus Christ alone is the one who has the authority to call and demand man to come to obedience. Bonhoeffer states, "Jesus is the Christ, he has authority to call and to demand obedience to his word. Jesus calls to discipleship, not as a teacher and a role model, but as the Christ, the Son of God."[259] The area of obedience is and apparently has always been a struggle for mankind. One can go back to the beginning of the Bible to the book of Genesis and visit the story of Adam and Eve. Sin entered the world as Eve disobeyed God followed closely by her man, Adam. Following that account of the sin of disobedience, in the

---

[258] Romans 3: 23
[259] Bonhoeffer, *Discipleship*, 57.

Bible are many stories of man standing in disobedience to God and His commandments. God is a loving God but He will chastise His children when they disobey as found in the book of Revelation, "As many as I love, I rebuke and chasten: be zealous therefore, and repent."[260] God calls mankind to obedience to His commandment, not for His power, but for man to live a life of love, joy, peace, and blessings of God. According to Watson and Watson, "It is clear from the words of Jesus and the writing of John that there can be no love for Christ without obedience to Christ.... The Bible teaches that obedience to the commands and teachings of God has direct benefit to those who believe. Sometimes these benefits are to the corporate body of Christ. Other times the benefits are personal and individual."[261] It is important to understand this point; man must love God and it is through this love that man desires to obey God. Man cannot manufacture this love for God as God loved man first. John makes this point as he says, "We love him, because he first loved us."[262] Man comes to this knowledge of love found only in Christ Jesus as John says, "Herein is love, not that we loved God, but that he loved us, and sent his Son to be the propitiation for our sins."[263] Man comes to His love first in the plan of salvation offered by God only in His Son Jesus Christ and once received, Jesus Christ dwells

---

[260] Revelation 3:19.
[261] Watson and Watson, *Contagious Disciple Making,* 40.
[262] 1 John 4:19.
[263] 1 John 4:10.

in man's heart. John makes this point as well as he says, "And we have known and believed the love that God hath to us. God is love; and he that dwelleth in love dwelleth in God, and God in him."[264]

Although John wrote the gospel of John to primarily the Jews, and ultimately the world, the works found in 1 John and his Epistles were written to stand against a radical and deviant form of Christianity called Gnosticism which taught that Jesus couldn't be the Messiah and attacked the plan of salvation. John was telling the world the truth of Jesus, His love, and how God truly loved the world. According to Andreas Kostenberger, "John's Gospel is an account of the life and ministry of Jesus… the Epistles deal with an early Gnostic threat to already established Christian communities."[265] It is clear that not only did John stand against this form of false teaching; his desire was to share the love of God, in and through, Jesus Christ, with the world. Jesus teaches that man must be reborn into the family of God, abide in Him and obey the commandments of God. Jesus speaks of this as He says, "I am the vine, ye are the branches: He that abideth in me, and I in him, the same bringeth forth much fruit: for without me ye can do nothing."[266] Merrill Tenney states, "The first and most important relationship which the disciples should maintain was with Jesus. In order to

---

[264] 1 John 4:16.

[265] Andreas J. Kostenberger, *Encountering John: The Gospel in Historical, Literary, and Theological Perspective* (Grand Rapids, MI: Baker Academic, 1999), 205.

[266] John 15:5.

enforce its meaning, He used the allegory of the vine."[267] Jesus continues as He says in the book of John, "If ye keep my commandments, ye shall abide in my love; even as I have kept my Father's commandments, and abide in His love."[268] Elmer Town's states, "….there is an indissoluble bond linking our love for Christ and our subsequent willingness to obey and keep His commandments."[269] Obedience to the keeping of the commandments of God gives evidence that one has love for God.

Also, a man should serve God because he desires to obey Him. Moses spoke to this in Deuteronomy as he said, "Ye shall walk after the Lord your God, and fear him, and keep his commandments, and obey his voice, and ye shall serve him, and cleave unto him."[270] Moses gives clear evidence that man must love God and through this love one will serve Him and keep His commandments. Whitney says, "Everything in that verse relates to obedience to God. During this cluster of commands on obedience is the mandate, "serve Him." We should serve the Lord because we want to obey Him."[271]

---

[267] Merrill C. Tenney, *John – The Gospel of belief: An Analytic Study of The Text* (Grand Rapids, MI: William B. Eerdmans Publishing Company, 1976), 226.

[268] John 15:10.

[269] Elmer L. Towns, *The Gospel of John: Believe and Live: A Verse-By-Verse Bible Study Commentary* (Grand Rapids, MI: Revel Publishing, 1990), 276.

[270] Deuteronomy 13: 4.

[271] Whitney, *Spiritual Disciplines for The Christian Life*, 118.

Chapter 15

My Hope

"But they that wait upon the Lord shall renew
their strength; they shall mount up with wings
as eagles; they shall run, and not be weary;
and they shall walk, and not faint."
Isaiah 40: 31

Again, let me be clear – *I LOVE GOD'S CHURCH! I
HATE WHAT MAN HAS DONE TO GOD'S CHURCH*!
The closest I can come to explaining this is that I love the
sinner and hate the sin! This world continues to spiral
into the depths of a wickedness unknown to man because
the church is dying. Prior to our present age, the United
States of America followed the church. The American
Church was the moral compass for an entire country. The
American Church led the way to a brighter future and the
country followed for many generations. However, as the
American Church gasps for her last breath, so it is with
the United States of America gasping for her last breath.

Being honest, Satan has been attacking the church since

the time of Jesus. He wanted, and still wants, the church to die just like he wanted Jesus to die. We must remember that Jesus is the King! One of my favorite scriptures in John 10: 10, "The thief cometh not, but for to steal, and to kill, and to destroy: I am come that they might have life, and that they might have it more abundantly." Satan comes to kill the church and to destroy it, but Jesus comes to give *LIFE*! We must Awake and Arise and turn to Jesus in all ways and find our *LIFE*! The American Church *can* find her life if she is willing to return in humbleness and be blessed by the King!

We as a Godly people must stand up under the banner of Jesus Christ and fight like we have never fought before and bring revival to our churches. If you are sitting on a leadership board of a church – you must make a stand to lead the church in a Biblical manner and stop trying to please man. We live in a time of consumerism and the church has fallen prey to this disease. The leadership boards of our churches are trying to please the consumers of their community and attempting to lower the bar to draw more consumers to their church to purchase their product. That was never God's plan and it was never God's way. Stand in the truth and lead under the power of the Holy Spirit for if you don't, there will be a time you will regret ever serving on that board.

If you are a pastor of a local church and you won't bring the gospel of Jesus Christ, you must ask yourself, why? Could it be you are in the business of religion and only want to get paid? Are you not called by God to serve God by serving the flock that He gave you? Are you in fear that if you stand up and take the side of God and preach His truth that the leadership board will fire you? What ever the reasons for the weak preachers we have in the American Church, if you are a pastor – Stand up for the truth and reject the fear of man and begin to fear God. This is one aspect of the American Church that is on trial. As we continue to proceed down this path, we choose to reject the fear of God. This fear of God is a Biblical fear and it means to respect God for who He is and for all He is. There should be a healthy respect to fear the wrath of God as He is beginning to show His great displeasure in man in the destruction of His church. As a pastor – stand up or get out!

> "Preach the word; be instant in season, out of season; reprove, rebuke, exhort with all long-suffering and doctrine. For the time will come when they will not endure found doctrine; but after their own lusts shall they heap to themselves teachers, having itching ears; And they shall turn away their ears from the truth, and shall be turned unto fables. But watch thou in all things, endure afflictions, do the work of an evangelist, make full proof of thy ministry" 2 Timothy 4:2-5

To the congregations of the American Church – I bring this charge to you. Are you a congregation that only wants to hear soft, sweet, feel-good messages from your leaders and if they deviate from that plan, you will threaten to leave the church or have the pastor/leader fired and find a person who will do as *you* wish. In the above scripture did you catch what was being said about you? "they shall turn away their ears from the truth and shall be turned unto fables." Are your ears itchy and do you reject the truth found only in the person of Jesus Christ and in the Bible – the true word of God? Are you standing in your own power to get what you want instead of bowing to the power and the person of God the Holy Spirit? If you are, before it is to late, stand up as the body of Christ and bring Him glory. Stand up and make your statement that you will accept and rejoice in the power of the Holy Spirit in His church and reject any leader or pastor that doesn't agree with you. There is power in numbers and there are numbers in your church that want change. Many congregations suffer from only attending church to be social or religious. If that is you – leave His church immediately and do not bring any wrath of God on yourself but repent of this and go to church to worship God only!

My hope, my most sincere hope, is that this book will move others to not only come to the truth of what we have done to His church but be moved to know that God always blesses His people who repent and desire forgiveness for their past. It is not too late for all who have not repented and confessed the sins of being a part of the destruction of His church to turn and allow God to make a way back to the light.

I love you and I love God's Church! I pray we will not be the generation that is charged by God with the legacy of destruction. May God bless you and your family, may God bless the United States of America, and may God bless His Church.

Bibliography

Anderson, Leith. *The Jesus Revolution: Learning from Christ's First Followers.* Nashville, TN: Abingdon Press. 2009.

Arnold, Jeffrey. *The Big Book on Small Groups.* Downers Grove, IL: InterVarsity Press. 1992.

Barclay, William. The Revelation of John. Volume 1 (Chapters 1 to 5). Revised Ed. Philadelphia, PA: The Westminster Press. 1976.

Barna, George and David Kinnaman. Gen. Ed. *Churchless: Understanding Today's Unchurched and How to Connect with Them.* Carol Stream, IL: Tyndale Momentum. 2014.

Barna, George. *Growing True Disciples: New Strategies for Producing Genuine Followers of Christ.* Colorado Springs, CO: WaterBrook Press. 2001.

Barna, George. *Marketing the Church*, Colorado Springs, CO: NavPress. 1990.

Beard, Christopher. "Missional discipleship: discerning spiritual-formation practices and goals within the missional movement." *Missiology, Apr 2015.*

Beckham, William. *The Two-Winged Church Will Fly.* Houston, TX: Touch Publications. 1993.

Benner, David G. *Surrender to Love: Discovering the Heart of Christian Spirituality.* Downers Grove, IL: InterVarsity Press. 2003.

Bonhoeffer, Dietrich. *Discipleship.* Minneapolis, MN: First Fortress Press. 2003.

Brooks, K. H. *Addressing apathy in the church: Moving people towards a biblical healthy discipleship model* (Order No. 3636361). Available from Dissertations & Theses @ Liberty University. 2014.

Bruce, F.F. The Hard Sayings of Jesus. Downers Grove, IL: InterVarsity Press. 1983.

Buchanan, Rodney. *History of Pre-Reformation Small Groups.* Article used by Dr. Dempsey at Liberty University Class. 2015.

Carlson, Kent and Mike Lueken, *Renovation of the Church.* Downers Grove, IL: InterVarsity Press. 2011.

Carson. D. A. *The Gospel According to John: The Pillar New Testament Commentary.* Grand Rapids, MI: Eerdmans Publishing Company. 1991.

Cashmore, David. "Laodicea and the seven churches." *Stimulus* 12, no. 2 (May 2004): 16-20.

Cole, Neil. *Church 3.0: Upgrades for the future of the church.* San Francisco, CA: Jossey-Bass. 2010.

Cole, Neil. *Organic Leadership: Leading Naturally Right Where You Are.* Grand Rapids, MI: Baker Books. 2009.

Cole, Neil. *Organic Church: Growing Faith Where Life Happens.* San Francisco, CA: Jossey-Bass. 2005.

Cole, Neil and Phil Helfer. *Church Transfusion: Changing Your Church Organically from the Inside Out.* San Francisco, CA: Jossey-Bass. 2012.

Coleman, Robert E. *The Master Plan of Evangelism.* 2nd. ed. Grand Rapids, MI: Revell Publishing. 1993.

Comiskey, Joel. *The Joel Comiskey Group.* http://www.joelcomiskeygroup.com/articles/dissertation/History.html. 2015.

Dickson, John. *Humilitas: A Lost Key to Life, Love, and Leadership.* Grand Rapids, MI: Zondervan. 2011.

Dillenberger, John. *Martin Luther: Selections from His Writings.* New York, NY: Anchor Books. 1962.

Donahue, Bill and Russ Robinson. *Building A Church of Small Groups: a place where nobody stands alone.* Grand Rapids, MI: Zondervan. 2001.

Earley, Dave. *Prayer: The Timeless Secret of High-Impact Leaders.* Chattanooga, TN: Living Ink Books. 2008.

Earley, Dave and Rod Dempsey. 2013. *Disciple Making Is…: How to Live the Great Commission with Passion and Confidence.* Nashville, TN: B&H Publishing Group.

Earley, Dave and David Wheeler. 2010. *Evangelism Is…: How to Share Jesus with Passion and Confidence.* Nashville, TN: B&H Publishing Group.

Elwell, Walter, A. ed. 2001. *Evangelical Dictionary of Theology.* 2nded. Grand Rapids, MI: Baker Academic.

Erickson, Millard J. Christian Theology. 2nd ed. Grand Rapids, MI: Baker Academic. 1998.

Falwell, Jerry D. ed. *Liberty Bible Commentary: The Old-time Gospel Hour Edition.* Nashville, TN: Thomas Nelson, Inc. 1983.

Falwell, Jonathan. Ed. innovatechurch: Innovative leadership for the next generation church. Nashville, TN: B&H Publishing Group. 2008.

Fay, William and Linda Evans Shepherd. *Share Jesus Without Fear.* Nashville, TN: B&H Publishing Group. 1999. 11.

Ferguson, Everett. *Church History, Volume One: From Christ to Pre-Reformation.* Grand Rapids, MI: Zondervan. 2005.

Gordon, S. D. *Quiet Talks on Prayer. Shippensburg, PA: Destiny Image Publishing. 2003.*

Gorman, Julie. *Community That Is Christian: A Handbook on Small Groups.* Colorado Springs, CO: Chariot Victor. 1993.

Gould, William Blair. The Worldly Christian: Bonhoeffer on Discipleship. Philadelphia, PA: Fortress Press. 1967.

Graham, Franklin. July 8, 2016, e-mail message confirmation to author.

Graves, David E. "Jesus Speaks to Seven of His Churches, Part 2." Journal – Bible and Spade (Second Run) – Volume – BSPADE 23: 3 (Summer, 2010).

Greear, J.D. 2011. *Gospel: Recovering the Power that Made Christianity.* Nashville, TN: B&H Publishing Group.

Groothuis, Douglas. *Christian Apologetics: A Comprehensive Case for Biblical Faith.* Downers Grove, IL: InterVarsity Press. 2011.

Guthrie, D. ed. and J. A. Motyer, ed. 1287. *New Bible Commentary.* 3rd ed. Carmel, NY: B. Eerdmans Publishing Company. 1970.

Halley, Henry H. *Halley's Bible Handbook: An Abbreviated Bible Commentary. Revised Ed.* Grand Rapids, MI: Zondervan. 1965.

Herbst, Nate. *Great Commission Leadership: A workbook on Evangelism, Discipleship and Multiplying Christ-Like Multipliers.* Durango, CO: Master Plan Ministries. 2013.

Hewitt, Steven. Why the church is dying in America. *Christian Computing Magazine.* July 2012.

Hirsch, Alan. 2006. *The Forgotten Ways: reactivating the missional church.* Grand Rapids, MI: Baker Publishing Group.

Hirsch, Alan and Dave Ferguson. 2011. *On the verge: a journey into the apostolic future of the church.* Grand Rapids, MI: Zondervan.

Hood, Pat. *The Sending Church: The Church Must Leave the Building.* Nashville, TN: B&H Publishing Group. 2013.

Hull, Bill. *The Complete Book of Discipleship: On Being and Making Followers Of Christ.* Colorado Springs, CO: NavPress. 2006.

Icenogle, Garth Weldon. *Biblical Foundations for Small Group Ministry: An Integrational Approach.* Downers Grove, IL: InterVarsity Press. 1994.

Jacques, Ellul. *Apocalypse: The Book of Revelation.* New York, NY: Seabury. 1977.

Johnson, Benton, Dean R Hoge, and Donald A. Luidens. "Mainline Churches: The Real Reason for Decline." First Things 31, (March 1993): 13-18. ATLA Religion Database with ATLASerials, EBSCOhost (accessed July 5, 2016).

Johnson, Judy. *Good Things Come in Small Groups: The Dynamics of Good Group Life.* Downers Grove, IL: InterVarsity Press. 1985.

Kent Carlson and Mike Lueken. Renovation of the Church. Downers Grove, IL: InterVarsity Press. 2011.

Kiddle, Martin and M. K. Ross. *The Revelation of St. John*. New York, NY: Harper & Brothers Publishers. 1941.

Koessler, John. *True Discipleship: The Art of Following Jesus*. Chicago, IL: Moody Publishers. 2003.

Kostenberger, Andreas J. *Encountering John: The Gospel in Historical, Literary, and Theological Perspective*. Grand Rapids, MI: Baker Academic. 1999.

Ladd, George Eldon. *A Commentary on the Revelation of John*. Grand Rapids, MI: Wm. B. Eerdmans Publishing Co. 1972.

Lancaster, Daniel B. *Making Radical Disciples*. Gardena, CA: T4T Press. 2011.

Larry Alex Taunton, "Listening to young Atheists: Lessons for a Stronger Christianity," The Atlantic, June 6, 2013, http://www.theatlantic.com/national/archive/2013/06/listening-to-young-atheists-lessons-for-a-stronger-christianity/276584/.

Lindsey, Hal. *There's A New World Coming: A Prophetic Odyssey*. Santa Ana, CA: Vision House Publishers. 1973.

MacArthur, John. *Pastoral Ministry: How to Shepherd Biblically*. Nashville, TN: Thomas Nelson, Inc. 2005.

MacArthur, John. *Preaching: How to Preach Biblically*. Nashville, TN: Thomas Nelson, Inc. 2005.

Mallison, John. *Growing Christians in Small Groups*. Homebush West, N.S.W: ANZEA Publishers. 1989.

Map. *The Seven Churches of Revelation*. BibleStudy.Org. http://www. biblestudy.org/maps/the-seven-churches-of-revelation-map. html.

McRay, John. *Archaeology & The New Testament*. Grand Rapids, MI: Baker House Company. 1997.

Mish, Frederick C. Ed. *Webster's Ninth New Collegiate Dictionary*. Springfield, MA: Merriam-Webster, Inc. Publishers. 1990.

Mitchell, Michael R. *Leading, Teaching, and Making Disciples: World-Class Christian Education in the church, School, and Home*. Bloomington, IN: Cross Books. 2010.

Moreau, A. Scott, Gary R. Corwin and Gary B. McGee. *Introducing World Missions: A Biblical, Historical and Practical Survey*. Grand Rapids, MI: Baker Academic Publishing. 2004.

Morris, Leon. *1 Corinthians. Tyndale New Testament Commentaries*. Grand Rapids, MI: Eerdmans. 1958.

Myers Allen C. ed. *The Eerdmans Bible Dictionary*. Grand Rapids, MI: William B. Eerdmans Publishing Company. 1987.

Nicholas, Ron and a Small Group. 1985. *Good Things Come in Small Groups: The Dynamics of Good Group Life*. Downers Grove, IL: InterVarsity Press.

Ogden, Greg. 2003. *Transforming Discipleship: Making Disciples a Few at a Time*. Downers Grove, IL: InterVarsity Press.

Ortberg, John. *The me I want to be: becoming God's best version of you*. Grand Rapids, MI: Zondervan. 2010.

Overstreet, R. L. "The Temple of God in the Book of Revelation." *Bibliotheca Sacra* 166, no. 664 (2009).

Platt, David. *Radical: Taking Your Faith Back from the American Dream.* Colorado Springs, CO: Multnomah, 2010.

Putman, Jim. *Real-life discipleship: building churches that make disciples.* Colorado Springs, CO: NavPress. 2010.

Rainer, Thom. The unchurched next door: Understanding Faith Stages as Keys to Sharing Your Faith. Grand Rapids, MI: Zondervan. 2003.

Rainer, Thom. *Autopsy of a Deceased Church: 12 Ways to keep yours Alive.* Nashville, TN: B&H Publishing Group, 2014

Rainer, Thom S. and Eric Geiger. *Simple Church: Returning to God's Process for Making Disciples.* Nashville, TN: B&H Publishing Group. 2011.

Rankin, Jerry. 2009. *Spiritual Warfare: The Battle for God's Glory.* Nashville, TN: B&H Publishing Group.

Reddish, Mitchell G. *Smyth & Helwys Bible Commentary: Revelation.* Macon, GA: Smyth & Helwys Publishing, Inc. 2001.

Richards, Lawrence O. *The Teacher's Commentary: Explains and Applies the Scriptures In A Way That Will Help You Teach Any Lesson From Genesis To Revelation.* Colorado Springs, CO: Scripture Press Publications. 1987.

Ryrie, Charles C. *The Holy Spirit. Revised and Expanded.* Chicago, IL: Moody Publishers. 1997.

Sanchez. Daniel, R. 2007. *Church Planting Movements in North America.* Fort Worth, TX: Church Starting Network.

Scazzero, Peter. 2010. *The Emotionally healthy Church: A Strategy for Discipleship that Actually Changes Lives.* Grand Rapids, MI: Zondervan.

Schultz, Thom and Joani Schultz. *Why Nobody Wants to Go to Church Anymore: And How 4 Acts of Love Will Make your Church Irresistible.* Loveland, CO: Group. 2013.

Sidey, Ken. "Church Growth Fine Tunes its Formulas," *Christianity Today,* (June 24, 1991).

Smith, Steve and Ying Kai. *A Discipleship ReRevolution: T4T.* Monument, CO: WIG Take Resources. 2011.

Smither, Edward L. *Augustine as Mentor. A Model for Preparing Spiritual Leaders.* Nashville, TN: B&H Publishing Group. 2008.

Spurgeon, Charles. *Lectures to My Students: Complete and Unabridged.* Grand Rapids, MI: Zondervan. 1954.

Stanford, Miles J. *The Complete Green Letters.* Grand Rapids, MI: Zondervan. 1983.

Stark, Rodney. 2011. *The Triumph of Christianity: How the Jesus Movement Became the World's Largest Religion.* New York, NY: HarperCollins Publishers.

Stowell, Joseph M. *Redefining Leadership: Character-Driven Habits of Effective Leaders.* Grand Rapids, MI: Zondervan. 2014.

T. Clegg and T. Bird, *Lost in America* (Loveland, CO: Group Publishing, 2001).

Taunton, Larry Alex, Listening to young Atheists: Lessons for a Stronger Christianity, *The Atlantic,* June 6, 2013, http://www. theatlantic.com/national/archive/2013/06/listening-to-young-atheists-lessons-for-a-stronger-christianity/276584/.

Tenney, Merrill C. *Interpreting Revelation.* Grand Rapids, MI: Wm. B. Eerdmans Publishing Company. 1957.

Tenney, Merrill C. *John – The Gospel of belief: An Analytic Study of The Text.* Grand Rapids, MI: William B. Eerdmans Publishing Company. 1976.

Thumma, Scott. A health Checkup of U. S. Churches by Hartford institute for Religion Research. (presentation, Future of the Church Summit from Group Publishing, Loveland, CO, October 22, 2012.

Thumma, Scott and Dave Travis. *Beyond Megachurch Myths: What We Can Learn from America's Largest Churches.* San Francisco, CA: Jossey-Bass Publishers. 2007.

Towns, Elmer L. *Praying the Lord's Prayer for Spiritual Breakthrough: Daily Praying the Lord's Prayer as A Pathway into His Presence.* Ventura, CA: Regal Books. 1997.

Towns, Elmer L. *Fasting for Spiritual Break Through: A Guide to Nine Biblical Fasts.* Ventura, CA: Regal Books. 1996.

Towns, Elmer. *The Gospel of John: Believe and Live: A Verse-By-Verse Bible Study Commentary.* Grand Rapids, MI: Revel Publishing. 1990.

Tyson, Jon. *Sacred Roots: Why the Church Still Matters.* Grand Rapids, MI: Zondervan. 2013.

Vine, W. E., Merrill F. Unger, and William White, Jr. *Vine's Complete Expository Dictionary of Old and New Testament Words.* Nashville, TN: Thomas Nelson Publishers. 1985.

Vine, W. E., Merrill F. Unger, and William White, Jr. *Vine's Complete Expository Dictionary of Old and New Testament words.* Nashville, TN: Thomas Nelson Publishers. 1996.

Viola, Frank. *Reimagining Church: Pursuing the Dream of Organic Christianity.* Colorado Springs, CO: David C. Cook Publishing. 2008.

Walvoord, John. *The Revelation of Jesus Christ: A Commentary by John F. Walvoord.* Chicago, IL: Moody Press. 1966.

Walvoord, John F. *The Holy Spirit.* 3rd ed. Grand Rapids, MI: Zondervan. 1966.

Walvoord, John F. and Roy Zuck. *The Bible Knowledge Commentary: An Exposition of the Scriptures by Dallas Seminary Faculty.* Wheaton, IL: Victor Books. 1983.

Watson, David L. and Paul D. Watson. *Contagious Disciple Making: Leading Others on a Journey of Discovery.* Nashville, TN: Thomas Nelson. 2014.

Whitney, Donald S. *Spiritual Disciplines for The Christian L.I.F.E.* Colorado Springs, CO: NavPress. 1991.

Wilkes, C. Gene. *Jesus On Leadership: Discovering the secrets of servant leadership.* Carol Stream, IL: Tyndale House Publishers, Inc. 1998.

Willard, Dallas. *Discipleship. http://www.dwillard.org/articles/artview. asp?artID=134.* Article for the Oxford Handbook of Evangelical Theology, edited by Gerald McDermott, 2010. 5.

Willmington, Harold L. *Willmington's Guide to the Bible. Vol. 2 New Testament.* Wheaton, IL: Tyndale House Publishers. 1986.

Zempel, Heather. *Models of Discipleship Throughout Church History.* http://discipleshipgroups.blogspot.com/2006/02/models-of-discipleship-throughout.html. 2006.

Printed in the United States
By Bookmasters